# Religion in Criminal Justice

# Religion in Criminal Justice

Monica K. Miller

LFB Scholarly Publishing LLC
El Paso, Texas, 2008

First published 2006 by LFB Scholarly Publishing LLC.
First printing in paperback, 2008.
All rights reserved.


Library of Congress Cataloging-in-Publication Data

Miller, Monica K.
  Religion in criminal justice / Monica K. Miller.
    p. cm. -- (Criminal justice (LFB Scholarly Publishing LLC))
  Includes bibliographical references and index.
  ISBN 1-59332-142-2 (alk. paper)
  1. Summation (Law)--United States. 2. Jury--United States. 3. Capital
punishment--United States. 4. Religion and law--United States. I.
Title.
II. Series.
  KF8924.M55 2006
  347.73'75--dc22

                                        2006006302



ISBN 978-1-59332-142-0 (casebound)
ISBN 978-1-59332-337-0 (paperback)


Printed on acid-free 250-year-life paper.
Manufactured in the United States of America.

# Table of Contents

# Acknowledgements

First and foremost, I would like to thank Kevin for his support and understanding. This would not be possible without you! Thanks to Brian Bornstein, Rich Weiner, Dick Dienstbier and Bob Schopp for their guidance throughout the course of this project. I would also like to thank the editorial staff of Law and Psychology Review for their helpful editing of the sections that were previously published in their journal.

Thanks also to a long, long list of research assistants, especially Beth Herschlag, who helped me with this project. I also owe a special thanks to Stacy Norbeck for helping preparing the manuscript for publication. Finally, I am indebted to the faculty at the University of Nevada, Reno for their support and patience!

This research was supported by grants from the National Science Foundation (NSF), the Society for the Psychological Study of Social Issues (SPSSI), and the American Psychology -Law Society (AP-LS). The financial support of the University of Nebraska is also gratefully acknowledged.

# CHAPTER 1

# An Introduction to Religion in Criminal Justice

In a criminal court in Virginia, a lawyer asks potential jurors to reveal their religious preferences, what religion they were raised to follow, how often they attend religious services, and whether they are familiar with Islamic practices (Blum, 2005).[1] While these questions might seem odd in most criminal cases, they are of utmost importance in the trial of Ali Al-Timimi, an American citizen accused of supporting terrorism. Lawyers in cases such as this are relying on the jury selection process to help them pick jurors that are the most sympathetic to their side. In doing so, lawyers use information about a potential juror's religiosity to predict whether the juror will be predisposed to find the defendant guilty or not guilty.

Another lawyer, making closing arguments in a death penalty sentencing trial, tells jurors "Let's get down to what this trial and what the laws are all about...this is retribution. An eye for an eye. A tooth for a tooth. Right there in the Bible... How do we put it now? Let the punishment fit the crime (Greene v. State p 147)." This religious appeal is the prosecutor's attempt to convince the jury to sentence the defendant to death.

---

[1] Sections of this text originally appeared in Miller, M. K. & Bornstein, B. H. (2005). Religious Appeals in Closing Arguments: Impermissible Input or Benign Banter? *Law and Psychology Review, 29,* 29-61. Reprinted with permission.

Judges have also allowed religion to influence their decisions. For instance, a judge in Kentucky gives the offenders he sentences the option of attending worship services instead of going to jail (Associated Press, May 31, 2005; Maimon, 2005). These are just a few examples of how religion is used in the court system. Despite the notion of "separation of church and state," a surprising number of lawyers and judges are bringing religion into the courtroom.

The Establishment Clause prohibits legal decisions from being made on religious grounds. While the judicial system often relies on resources from economics, psychology, sociology or history, reliance on religious resources is not allowed (Modak-Truran, 2004), even when religious texts can provide moral guidance that is potentially helpful in making legal decisions. This dilemma prompted author Steven Smith to call religion a "special kind of problem for the law" (Smith, 1998, p. 212).

Although there is concern about the use of religious appeals for many legal issues (e.g., abortion, gay rights, euthanasia, divorce, welfare, segregation, and war; see Blume and Johnson, 2000), and in many areas of the judicial system (e.g., the guilt phase, voir dire, jury deliberations, judicial sentencing procedures, and gubernatorial pardons; see Loewy, 2000; Simson & Garvey, 2001), this book will focus on the use of religious appeals by both prosecutors and defense attorneys during closing arguments in the sentencing phase of death penalty trials. Both prosecuting and defense attorneys can find Biblical support for their differing viewpoints (Hiers, 2004). While prosecutors typically rely on Biblical passages such as "an eye for an eye," defense attorneys point out passages that seemingly oppose the death penalty. Although some authors point out that Biblical passages are often misunderstood, they are used to suit these legal purposes (see, e.g., Hiers, 2004).

While religious appeals are used in many contexts, they may be particularly influential in death penalty trials. The Bible offers language that refers directly to the crime of murder (e.g., "thou shalt not kill" and "the murderer shall be put to death"), whereas the Bible does not offer such clearly relevant instruction regarding other crimes or disputes. Thus, it is especially useful to study the influence of religious appeals in the framework of death penalty trials.

Attorneys are allowed much freedom in their closing arguments (for a review, see Furman, 1995; Montz, 2001). Generally, attorneys are limited to the evidence offered at trial and the reasonable assumptions that can be drawn from that evidence; they must not express personal opinions or make arguments that appeal to the prejudices of the jury (ABA, 1993). Beyond these basic principles, the admissibility of attorney arguments, including the use of religious appeals, is left to the trial judge's discretion. Because religious appeals are not prohibited in most jurisdictions, attorneys who believe that appeals are persuasive may use them in their closing arguments.

Reliance on Biblical appeals has been promoted by Professor Gerald Uehlman, one of the members of the O.J. Simpson defense team, who has listed "Pound the Bible" as one of eight elements of a great closing argument (Wiehl, 2000). Though Uehlman is clearly a supporter of using the Bible as an advocacy tool, a nationwide survey of federal public defenders and prosecutors revealed that the majority of attorneys who responded had never referred to the Bible, and many were cautious about doing so because of the court's growing disapproval of such references (Wiehl, 2000). Although this seems to suggest that Biblical appeals are used infrequently, the author of the study admits the study was of anecdotal value only and was not intended to be of a scientific nature (Wiehl, 2000).[2] While it is difficult to determine how frequently religious appeals are used, legal discussions of relevant cases suggest that religious appeals are not infrequent and may even be growing in

---

[2] The study surveyed only Federal public defenders and prosecutors. The defenders were sent email surveys, to which only 10 defenders (17%) responded. The federal prosecutors were interviewed by the researcher, however sample size and response rate was not provided in the report.

frequency (Blume & Johnson, 2000; Brooks, 1999; Duffy, 1997; Henson, 2001; Loewy, 2000; Miller & Bornstein, 2005; Simons, 2004; Simson & Garvey 2001;Walker, 2003).

Chapter 2 will review the use of religion in recent high-profile cases in order to provide well-known illustrations of the use of religion in trials. Chapter 3 will provide a broader overview of the ways in which religion is used in many aspects of the court system. Next is a discussion of the religious appeals most commonly used by prosecuting and defense attorneys, followed by a review of the ways in which courts have reacted to the use of religious appeals. The results of two empirical research studies are presented in Chapters 9 and 10 in order to answer questions surrounding religious appeals. Results are presented as guidance for policy-makers and judges involved in the debate over religious appeals.

# CHAPTER 2

# Religion in High Profile Cases

Despite the notion of "separation of church and state," religion sneaks into every stage of a criminal justice trial. First, the defendant's religiosity can influence jurors, especially in cases where the defendant was a religious leader. Second, many crimes such as terrorist attacks have religious motives. Next, a defendant's mental health status is often questioned when he makes claims that God has directed him to commit the crime. Finally, religion can be used during jury selection, as evidence in the trial, or during attorney arguments. Although it is impossible to determine how many trials have involved the use of religion, a review of recent high-profile cases demonstrates that the use of religion is not uncommon.

## RELIGIOSITY OF THE DEFENDANT

Before a trial even starts, the defendant can begin shaping his image in order to make himself look more appealing to jurors. Portraying oneself as religious is one way to make jurors believe that one is a moral and decent person. For instance, Kobe Bryant, the professional basketball player accused of sexually assaulting a 19-year-old woman, used religion in this way (CNN.com, October 20, 2003). Before his criminal trial began, Bryant told the media, "I've pretty much done all I can here and, you know, God will carry me the rest of the way, so I'm pretty comfortable with that." Bryant's belief in God could have made him appear less deviant, possibly giving future jurors doubt that someone who believed in God could rape another person. Although Bryant's accuser decided not to follow through with a criminal trial, she is still pursuing a civil trial at the time of this writing.

Religious characteristics often play important roles in trials. For instance, some defendants have been leaders in their churches. Edgar Ray Killen, a former Ku Klux Klansman and Baptist preacher, was convicted in 2005 of manslaughter for the killings of three civil rights workers in 1964 (CNN.com, June 22, 2005). Similarly, Dennis Rader, the serial killer who referred to himself as BTK ("bind, torture and kill"), had been elected president of his Lutheran church council (CNN.com, June 28, 2005). Evidence of these defendants' religious participation was presented to jurors at trial.

Focusing on the religious characteristics of the defendant is not an isolated event. The Catholic church has come under fire in recent years, as charges of abuse have been brought to light. Between 1950 and 2002, about 4,400 Catholic priests nationwide have been accused of sexual abuse by over 10,000 people (Bailey, 2005).

Such characteristics can affect jurors in either of two ways. Jurors may feel that the person is likely being wrongly accused, as a follower of God would not commit such crimes. On the other hand, jurors could be more punitive towards the defendant than they would be if he was not a faithful believer of God. In such an instance, jurors may hold a believer to a higher standard of behavior (and punish him more) than a non-believer because the jurors think believers should not behave in such a sinful manner.

While some defendants are followers of common churches, others are members of more extreme religions. For example, Eric Rudolph, the "Olympics bomber" confessed to the bombings that occurred during the 1996 Olympics in Atlanta, Georgia (CNN.com, April 8, 2005). Rudolph followed white supremacist theology called Christian Identity. Rudolph was sentenced to life in prison in 2005. Although the case was not presented to a jury, it is likely that some jurors would have reacted negatively towards him because of his unorthodox religious beliefs.

Other defendants have been members of religions that many Americans characterize as anti-American.  For instance, John Allen Muhammad, one of the "Washington D.C. snipers," had converted to Islam and had even attended the Nation of Islam's Million Man March (CNN.com, October 24, 2002).  Similarly, John Walker Lindh, known as the Taliban American, had converted to Islam, attended an Islamic fundamentalist school, and supported the Jihad (i.e., the holy war; CNN.com, no date).

Jurors and judges are unlikely to be sympathetic to such defendants.  Muhammad was convicted and sentenced to death in 2003, while Walker Lindh pled guilty in 2002 and received 20 years in prison.  When jurors are faced with a defendants who belongs to a religion that is perceived as hostile to Americans, jurors may be more punitive towards the defendant than if he had belonged to a more traditional religion.

## RELIGIOUS MOTIVES

Religion motivates many defendants to commit their crimes.  Individuals like John Walker Lindh and Zacarias Moussaoui, the "twentieth hijacker," are examples of defendants who have religious motivations for committing crimes.  Moussaoui supported the September 11th attacks because of his strong religious beliefs (Dorf, 2005).  Similarly, Saajid Badat, the "British shoebomber," pled guilty in 2005 to planning a terrorist attack (Raif & Dean, 2005).  Badat had once declared his religious motivations by stating, "I have a sincere desire to sell my soul to Allah in return for paradise."

While religiously motivated terrorists such as those associated with the September 11th attacks are in the media forefront, religion also prompts other types of crimes.  In 2005, Zack Sinclair was convicted of stalking Mel Gibson after repeatedly attempting to pray with the actor

(Sweetingham, 2005; Associated Press, June 22, 2005). Eric Rudolph, the "Olympics bomber" also bombed abortion clinics because of his religious beliefs against abortion (Associated Press, July 18, 2005). In 2005, two 18-year old men pled guilty to the second-degree assault of a Church of Satan member (Grinberg, 2005). Such cases demonstrate a wide variety of religiously motivated crimes.

## RELIGION AS EVIDENCE OF MENTAL HEALTH

Religion is often offered as evidence that a defendant was insane or is mentally incompetent. In 2002, Andrea Yates was unsuccessful at convincing a jury that she was insane when she drown her five children in response God's instructions (CNN.com, March 13, 2002). In contrast, Deanna Laney was successful in convincing the jury that she was insane when she followed God's orders to stone her sons to death in 2003 (Springer, 2004). The next year, Dena Schlosser cut off her daughter's arms in an attempt to "give her child to God." Schlosser was found incompetent to stand trial (Associated Press, February 15, 2005).

In another recent example, Brian David Mitchell was found mentally incompetent to stand trial for the kidnapping of Elizabeth Smart (CNN.com, July 26, 2005). During several hearings in 2005, Mitchell was removed from the courtroom because he continuously sang hymns and yelled religious proclamations such as "Awaken, arise Israel. Come forth, Babylon. Repent, repent for the kingdom." At the time of this writing, Mitchell was confined to a mental health treatment center. If a future court determines that his mental health has improved enough to stand trial, he will face charges of kidnapping, sexual assault, and burglary.

## RELIGION IN THE TRIAL PROCESS

Once a case goes to trial, lawyers sometimes use the religion of potential jurors to help them decide which individuals to accept or reject. In the trial of the actor Robert Blake, lawyers asked potential jurors a number of questions about their  religiosity.  One juror was removed because she intended to make her verdict by praying, and another was excused for indicating that the verdict should be based on religious beliefs (Deutsch, 2004).  Jurors were questioned in detail about their religious beliefs in other famous cases, including those of sniper Lee Boyd Malvo (CNN.com, November 11, 2003), bomber Terry Nichols (*U.S. v. Nichols*, 1997), and terrorist Ali Al-Timimi (Blum, 2005).

Religion can also be used during the trial in a number of ways.  First, the defendant's behavior can suggest his religiosity.  In 2004, Jayson Williams, a former NBA player, was accused of shooting Costas Christofi (Ryan, 2004).  During the trial, Williams stated to the media "On the advice of my counsel, I will not testify.  I am innocent. I put my trust in God, and I have great confidence in this jury."  Williams also wore a cross on his suit jacket while in court.  These uses of religion indicate that Williams is a believer, a fact that has the potential to sway a jury.

Religion can also come in the form of evidence presented at trail.  Terry Nichols' lawyers presented evidence of Nichols' jailhouse conversion to Christianity as a way to convince the jury that he has "a great chance for redemption (Polk, 2004)."  Some jurors believed this was so, with one stating that some jurors, "thought he could do some good in prison because he found religion (CNN.com, June 12, 2004)."

The prosecution can also use religious evidence.  For instance, the prosecutor in the Ali Al-Timimi trial frequently used religious words with negative connotations (e.g., kafir, jihad, fatwa; Blum, 2005).  The prosecutor told the jurors that the defendant's belief in a militant Islamic religion was evidence of his criminal intent.  Further, the prosecutor argued that the defendant lied to the jury because he viewed jurors as enemies in his religious war.

Religion can also be found in attorneys' closing arguments.  The prosecutor in the Andrea Yates case said that Yates' behavior was "wrong in the eyes of God and it was wrong in the eyes of the law (CNN.com, March 13, 2002)." A defense attorney used a religious appeal in the case of John Taylor, who was accused of murdering workers in a New York Wendy's restaurant. He told the jurors "you have to look to your moral gods, whoever they are…wherever your sense of goodness and positive morality derives" in an attempt to convince the jurors to spare Taylor's life (Kershaw, 2002).

As these cases illustrate, religion is used in a variety of ways in the criminal justice system. From the moment a defendant is arrested, he can inject religion into the trial through his statements to the media. His religious beliefs and experiences can be brought up at trial as evidence of his character, his motives, or his mental state. Both attorneys can use religion in jury selection or during the trial. The number of high profile cases that contain religious components indicates that religion may be used frequently in courts across the country.

# CHAPTER 3

# Religion in the Legal System

As demonstrated by the review of high profile cases in Chapter 2, religion can impact the court system at any phase of the process (see also, Miller, Singer & Jehle, 2005). Lawyers can eliminate potential jurors based on their religiosity, defendants can present evidence that they have had a jailhouse conversion to Christianity, attorneys can offer Biblical guidance to jurors, and judges can let their own religiosity affect their decision-making.

Religion also affects the legal system outside of the trial process. For instance, religious beliefs of legal actors, such as governors, policymakers and the President, can affect the legal process. There is even some legal discussion about the role religion plays in the professional lives of attorneys (e.g., religious beliefs guiding the cases they pursue; Lesnick, 2002; Osler, 2005; Pearce & Uelmen, 2004). Such examples indicate that, despite a notion of "separation of church and state," religion plays an influential role in the legal system. While the high-profile examples in Chapter 2 provide well-known illustrations, a more in-depth legal and psychological analysis is needed to present a more complete picture of how religion affects every aspect of the legal system.

## RELIGION IN VOIR DIRE

During the early phases of a trial, lawyers and judges question potential jurors during the process of jury selection or "voir dire." During voir dire, potential jurors can be removed from the jury pool through several processes. Of most interest to this discussion is the process of removing potential jurors through the use of "peremptory challenges." Lawyers are given the chance to "challenge" (i.e., exclude from the jury) potential jurors who they feel will not be sympathetic to their side. For instance, a prosecutor may choose to remove a potential juror he feels will be sympathetic to the defendant.

The United State Supreme Court has determined that lawyers are allowed to use peremptory challenges to remove potential jurors for any reason, with the exception of race and gender (*Batson v. Kentucky*, 1986; *J.E.B. v. Alabama*, 1994). Thus, lawyers are free to remove jurors based on their religion, unless their state court prohibits such a challenge. Bornstein and Miller (2005) report that recent cases indicate a trend towards excluding potential jurors based on their religion. For instance, a California attorney challenged potential jurors who were Jewish, believing that Jews would be less likely to give the death penalty (CNN.com, March 21, 2005).

Prosecutors have challenged potential jurors because they possessed strong Christian beliefs (*U.S. v. DeJesus*, 2003) or had served as a missionary (*State v. Fuller*, 2004). Other prosecutors have challenged jurors who were Muslim (*State v. Fuller*, 2004), Catholic (*State v. Purcell*, 2001), Islamic (*State v. Hodge*, 2001), Jehovah's Witnesses (*People v. Martin*, 1998), and Pentecostal (*Casarez v. State*, 1995).

Because the Supreme Court has declined to issue a ruling on whether a peremptory challenge based on religion is permissible (*Davis v. Minnesota*, 1994), state courts have had to make their decisions independently. As a result of the lack of guidance from the Supreme Court, state courts have been divided on the issue (for review see, Bornstein & Miller, 2005; Mansfield, 2004; Waggoner, 2004). Some courts have allowed potential jurors to be removed because of their religion (*Casarez v. State*, 1995; *Minnesota v. Davis*, 1993) others have determined that such a practice is not acceptable (*State v. Eaton*, 1994; *State v. Fuller*, 2004; *State v. Purcell*, 2001; *Thornson v. State*, 1998). Others have made fine distinctions concerning when challenges can be made based on religiosity. For instance, two cases have allowed challenges based on degree of religiosity, but have forbid those based on religious affiliation (*U.S. v. DeJesus*, 2003; *State v. Hodge*, 2001). Until the United States Supreme Court rules on the issue, attorneys can use peremptory challenges to exclude potential jurors based on religion unless their state court has ruled otherwise.

Legal issues aside, there still exists some debate over whether using peremptory challenges to eliminate potential jurors on the basis of their religion is an effective way to choose a jury (Miller & Hayward, under review). Scientific studies of peremptory challenges suggest that individual difference variables do not affect trial outcomes as much as attorneys think they do (Diamond & Zeisel, 1974). Similarly, research on "scientific jury selection" has shown that selecting jurors based on demographic and attitudinal variables often yields little in the way of predictive validity (Fulero & Penrod, 1990). More specifically, research has pieced together an incomplete and uncertain picture of the relationship between religious factors and attitudes towards punishment, the death penalty, and verdicts. Because the relationship between religion and attitudes towards punishment is often uncertain, basing peremptory challenges on a person's religiosity may prove to be a futile effort.

The lawyer's ultimate goal during jury selection is to choose a jury that will be the most sympathetic to her client. Because religious teachings often provide instructions concerning appropriate punishment for sins, it seems logical that a potential juror's religious beliefs would predict whether they would support or oppose the death penalty. However, it is not that clear cut. Religion does not often strongly predict verdicts because religious beliefs tend to be very complex. While it is relatively simple to learn a juror's religion or even how faithfully they practice that religion, it is more difficult to measure more intricate beliefs such as a belief in a punitive God. Because religious beliefs derive from a complicated combination of denomination, devotionalism and individual interpretation, it becomes difficult to predict potential jurors' individual verdicts. Nevertheless, there has been some research that has shown that religiosity variables are related to beliefs about punishment, guilt verdicts, and sentencing verdicts (see generally Miller & Hayward, under review). These factors will be discussed in more detail in Chapter 7, however a brief discussion here will illustrate the various religious factors that may be related to jurors' verdicts and beliefs in punishment.

Some research has indicated that being particularly interested in religion, believing in a divine plan and purpose, and believing in life after death are related to a guilty vote (Howard & Redfering, 1983). Other studies have indicated that individuals who believe in a punitive God (Evans & Adams, 2003) and are religiously liberal (Vogel, 2003) tend to favor more severe punishments than their counterparts. Other religious characteristics such as religious ideology, fundamentalism, evangelism, devotionalism and literal interpretism are also related to views on punishment.

Religious denomination is related to attitudes towards punishment, as Catholics are less supportive of the death penalty than Protestants (Miller & Hawyard, under review; O'Neil, Patry & Penrod, 2004) and Jewish mock jurors were more lenient overall than Christians (Kerr, et. al, 1995).

The relationship between fundamentalism and attitudes towards punishment is somewhat murky. Although some research has found a positive relationship between religious fundamentalism and punitiveness or support for the death penalty (Grasmick, Cochran, Bursik & Kimpel, 1993; Grasmick, Davenport, Chamlin & Bursik, 1992; Young, 1992), other studies have not replicated this relationship

(Leiber & Woodrick, 1997; Miller & Hayward, under review). Similarly, the relationship between evangelism and the death penalty is equally unclear. Young (1992) found that evangelicals (i.e., individuals who have actively encouraged others to accept Jesus) are less likely to support the death penalty. On the other hand, other researchers have found that evangelicals are more punitive than their counterparts (Miller & Bornstein, under review; Songer and Tabrizi, 1999). Along with fundamentalism and evangelism, devotionalism does not have a clear relationship with punitiveness. Some studies indicate those high in devotionalism are less punitive (Bjarnason & Welch, 2004; Young, 1992), while another found that mock jurors who were highly devotional were more punitive (Johnson, 1985).

While many religious factors have produced unclear relationships with attitudes towards punishment, one factor has produced consistent (though limited) results. Individuals who believe that the Bible should be interpreted literally tend to be more punitive and more supportive of the death penalty than those individuals without that belief (Leiber & Woodrick, 1997; Miller & Bornstein, under review; Young, 1992).

Such studies indicate that the relationship between religiosity and attitudes towards punishment are very complicated, making the task of choosing which jurors to eliminate a difficult one. Some researchers have questioned whether eliminating jurors on the basis of religion violates common sense (Miller & Hayward, under review).

Miller & Hayward (under review) conducted a study to determine whether lawyers are correct in their assumptions that jurors' religiosity predicts their verdicts. Three studies were conducted to investigate these relationships. Two studies indicated that religious beliefs were related to death penalty attitudes. For instance, individuals who were skeptical of the death penalty (as opposed to those who were more supportive of the death penalty) were more likely to be Catholic, to believe that their religious beliefs were more important to their position on the death penalty, and to perceive their religious groups as less supportive of the death penalty. Skeptics tended to be more devotional, and less likely to interpret the Bible literally. Skeptics also believed that God is more forgiving and more merciful. On the other hand, death penalty supporters were more likely to believe that God supports or requires the death penalty for murderers. Miller and Hayward's third study revealed that attitudes towards the death penalty, literal interpretism, religious affiliation, gender, and the belief that God requires the death penalty for murderers predicted an individual's verdict. Based on these results, the authors concluded that lawyers should cautiously use religious information to pick a jury. Even though religious traits might not predict jurors' decisions perfectly, this method is likely a better method than simply using one's instincts or stereotypes (Miller & Hayward, under review).

## RELIGION AS EVIDENCE

In their role as advocates, lawyers raise arguments and offer religious evidence they believe will be the most persuasive to the jury. In doing so, both prosecuting and defense attorneys may rely on emotionally compelling religious arguments and evidence during the trial, encouraging jurors to use such religious instructions or imagery in their decision-making. As 96% of Americans believe in God (Gallup, 1995), it is plausible that many jurors could be influenced by evidence and arguments invoking God's instructions and guidance.

There are a number of ways religion can be introduced into evidence, either formally or informally (see generally, Miller, Singer & Jehle, 2005). First, parents accused of child abuse for refusing to seek medical treatment for their child may claim that their refusal was based on religious grounds. Second, some defendants may claim that they committed the crime because of religious delusions or hallucinations. Finally, defendants or attorneys may wear religious symbols during trial. For instance, Jayson

Williams wore a cross pin on his jacket while in the courtroom (CNN, 2004). Similarly, in the case of *La Rocca v. Lane* (1975), a Roman Catholic priest served as the defendant's attorney. Although the priest wanted to wear his clerical collar during the trial, the judge insisted the priest remove the collar, fearing that the jury would be biased by the religious symbol. Although there are many ways religion can be used as evidence, the focus here will be on the ways religion has been used as evidence in death penalty trials.

During the sentencing phase of a trial, attorneys present evidence of mitigating factors that are intended to convince the jury to spare the defendant's life. For instance, defense attorneys have argued that the defendant's religiosity indicates that the defendant is not deserving of the death penalty (*Boyd v. French*, 1998; *Brown v. Payton*, 2005; *Commonwealth v. Daniels*, 1994; *Crowe v. State*, 1995; *Miniel v. Cockrell*, 2003). Prison ministers, inmates, family, or prison employees can testify about the defendant's religiosity. Defendants' have presented evidence that they have converted to Christianity, established a prison ministry, or written Christian books (*Boyd v. French*, 1998; *Brown v. Payton*, 2005; *Commonwealth v. Cook*, 1996; *Commonwealth v. Daniels*, 1994; *Crowe v. State*, 1995; *Miniel v. Cockrell*, 2003). For example, in the case of *Brown v. Payton* (2005), defense witnesses testified that during the time that the defendant had been imprisoned, he had made an honest commitment to God and had joined a prison Bible study and prison ministry. The jury in this case did not feel that this behavior entitled Payton to a life sentence, and thus sentenced him to death. Payton challenged the sentence, arguing that the prosecutor improperly encouraged the jurors to ignore the conversion evidence. The U.S. Supreme Court ruled that the jury had likely considered the religious evidence but had found it unconvincing. The court stated, "Testimony about a religious conversion spanning one year and nine months may well have been considered altogether insignificant in light of the brutality of the crimes (p. 1442)."

Anecdotal evidence supports the notion that such religious evidence is, at least sometimes, successful. For example, in the sentencing trial of Terry Nichols, the co-conspirator in the Oklahoma City bombing, the defense attorney presented evidence that Nichols had converted to Christianity after his crimes. Some jurors "thought he could do some good in prison because he found religion" and thus refused to support a death sentence (CNN.com, June 12, 2004). The result was a hung jury, which essentially saved Nichols' life.

The courts have generally been supportive of the introduction of such testimony and argument, as it is evidence of the defendant's character (*Commonwealth v. Daniels*, 1994). This ruling is consistent with the Supreme Court's ruling that defendants have the right to produce evidence in mitigation (*Lockett v. Ohio*, 1978).

While there is little legal debate about the use of religion in the sentencing phase of death penalty trials, the issue has led to some discussion and debate by various scholars. In example, Simons (2004) argues that jailhouse conversions do not automatically persuade the jury to be more lenient. A simple claim that the defendant has found religion is not likely to be persuasive enough to convince a jury; the defendant should also repent and accept responsibility for his crime.

Other scholars have empirically studied the use of religion in trials. An early study manipulated the use of a religious appeal and found that jurors were more likely to convict a defendant when he used evidence of his religiosity as a defense in a child abuse trial as compared to when he did not use such evidence (Johnson, 1985). In addition, defendants who used religion in their defense were perceived as more responsible for their crimes, were more likely to be found guilty and received longer sentences compared to defendants who did not offer religious evidence. These results indicate that religious appeals may backfire. Johnson speculated that jurors expect Christian individuals to be morally responsible.

Because the defendant violated this expectation by harming others, mock jurors became angry when the defendant later used his religiosity as a reason to get a lighter sentence.

Simons (2004) agrees that evidence of a defendant's religiosity can have the opposite effect as intended. Specifically, jurors who are not themselves religious are likely to be uncomfortable when hearing this religious evidence. Additionally, jurors who are prejudiced towards the defendant's religion could form a negative impression of the defendant because of his religiosity.

While Johnson (1985) found that being a Christian defendant led jurors to be more punitive, a study by Miller and Bornstein (under review) revealed that being a lifelong Christian did not affect verdicts. Mock jurors did not show the defendant leniency simply because he claimed to be a Christian. Instead, they treated religious defendants the same as when defendants who did not use religion in their defense.

However the same study found that evidence of a jailhouse conversion did affect verdicts (Miller& Bornstein, under review). This study presented mock jurors with a stimuli of a death penalty sentencing trial. One of the following religious appeals were included: 1) the defendant had always been a Christian, 2) the defendant had converted to Christianity while imprisoned, 3) the defense attorney gave a Biblical appeal during closing arguments or 4) religion was not used in the trial. The researchers also manipulated whether or not the prosecutor gave a religious appeal during the closing arguments and the severity of the crime (manipulated by varying the number of aggravators and mitigators). When the defendant presented evidence of his religious conversion, he was treated the least punitively of all groups. The authors speculated that mock jurors believed that the defendant had changed for the better and was now able to be a more productive and positive person. Although the evidence is sparse and somewhat unclear, it is possible that a defendant's religiosity could persuade jurors and influence verdicts.

## RELIGION IN CLOSING ARGUMENTS

Attorneys in numerous cases have used religious appeals in closing arguments (e.g., *Boyd v. French*, 1998; *Brown v. Payton*, 2005; *Carruthers v. State*, 2000; *Christenson v. State*, 2004; *Commonwealth v. Chambers*, 1991; *Commonwealth v. Daniels*, 1994; *People v. Harrison*, 2005; *Sandoval v. Calderon*, 2000; *State v. Phillips*, 1997; *State v. Richardson*, 1998; *State v. Roache*, 2004). Prosecutors who use Biblical appeals in the sentencing phase of death penalty trials commonly rely on a Biblical passage referring to "an eye for an eye." Applied to the defendant, this passage suggests that jurors should sentence the defendant to death because he killed another person. Meanwhile, defense attorneys commonly quote a Biblical passage in which Jesus states, "You have heard that it [has been] said '[an] eye for an eye and [a] tooth for [a] tooth; but I say to you . . . [i]f someone strikes you on the right cheek, turn... the other also (Matthew, NIV 5: 38-9)." Such arguments are discussed in greater detail in Chapters 4 and 5.

The legal response to the use of religion in closing arguments has been quite varied (see, e.g., Miller & Bornstein, 2005). Courts that are the most restrictive have prohibited all appeals (e.g., *Commonwealth v. Chambers*, 1991; *Commonwealth v. Cook*, 1996; *Commonwealth v. Daniels*, 1994; *Sandoval v. Calderon*, 2000). More lenient courts have accepted religious appeals. For example, some have determined that appeals are within the boundaries of a lawyer's poetic license (*Bussard v. Lockhard*, 1994; *Commonwealth v. Henry*, 1990; *Commonwealth v. Whitney*, 1986). Less extreme courts have developed rules that guide the use of religious appeals. In example, courts have determined that appeals are acceptable if they are not excessive (*State v. Debler*, 1993; *State v. Phillips*, 1997), do not extend beyond providing evidence of the defendant's character (*Commonwealth v. Daniels*, 1994; *State v. Cauthern*, 1996), are not targeted at jurors' prejudice (*Cunningham v. Zant*, 1991), are not overly offensive (*State v. Ramsey*, 1993), and do not argue that

Biblical law requires a certain outcome (*People v. Harrison*, 2005). These court decisions are discussed in greater detail in Chapter 6.

While the use of the religion in the courts has garnered the attention of the legal community (see, e.g., Blume & Johnson, 2000; Brooks, 1999; Duffy, 1997; Henson, 2001; Loewy, 2000; Miller & Bornstein, 2005; Simons, 2004; Simons, 2004; Simson & Garvey 2001;Walker, 2003), the practice has received relatively little empirical attention.

The Miller and Bornstein (under review) study is the only known study investigating the use of religious appeals in closing arguments. As discussed above, the study manipulated the type of prosecution appeal, defense appeal, and the number of aggravators and mitigators present in the case facts. Results indicated that a Biblical appeal given by the prosecutor during closing arguments did not have any effect on mock jurors' verdicts. However Biblical appeals offered by the defense did affect verdicts. When the defense attorney presented a Biblical appeal, jurors were the most punitive, especially when there were more mitigators and fewer aggravators (indicating a less severe crime). Thus, an appeal by a defense attorney during closing arguments actually backfired and led to more death sentences.

Courts have also been concerned that religious appeals interfere with jurors' abilities to weigh aggravators and mitigators, as required by law (e.g., *Carruthers v. State*, 2000; *Sandoval v. Calderon*, 2000). The Miller and Bornstein (under review) study also investigated this concern. While prosecution appeals did not affect the ability to weigh aggravators and mitigators, defense appeals did. Specifically, when jurors did not receive any religious appeal or when they read that the defendant had converted to Christianity, they were able to weigh aggravators and mitigators properly. However, when jurors read that the defendant had always been a Christian or when they heard a Biblical appeal from the defense lawyer, they were unable to properly weigh aggravators and mitigators. Thus, some types of religious appeals improperly affect jurors' decision-making.

RELIGION IN DELIBERATIONS

Jurors have also relied on religious beliefs during their deliberations (*Colorado v. Harlan*, 2005). In the most recent and notable case, jurors in a death penalty sentencing trial brought a Bible into the deliberation room and researched Biblical passages (Pankratz, 2005), including the passage stating that murders should be punished "an eye for an eye and to tooth for a tooth" (Lindsay, 2003; Paulson, 2005). The District Judge overturned the death sentence, determining that jurors inappropriately relied on Biblical passages (Lindsay, 2003). This decision was upheld by the Colorado Supreme Court (Paulson, 2005). Finally, the U.S. Supreme Court denied certiorari in the case (*Colorado v. Harlan*, 2005). Thus, some courts have determined that it is impermissible for jurors to rely on the Bible in their deliberations.

Some authors find it inappropriate to allow jurors to rely on the Bible and other religious texts because these writings are inconsistent and can be translated in contradicting ways (Egland, 2004). Because the Bible offers passages that seemingly promote the death penalty, while others seemingly promote forgiveness, even jurors of the same religion could come to differing conclusions (Egland, 2004; Hiers, 2004). Further concerns involve the limits of what texts can be used in deliberation. If Bibles are allowed in the courtroom, should other religious texts be allowed as well? What about Philosophical texts, such as that by Gandhi, which promote forgiveness and peace (Egland, 2004)? Thus, it is difficult to know where to draw the line. Ultimately, a strict line could be drawn so that no non-legal source could be allowed during deliberations. This would not fully address the problem, however, as jurors could still quote passages from memory or privately rely on these religious teachings.

## RELIGION IN JUDICIAL DECISIONS

In addition to the variety of ways lawyers and jurors have used religion, judges have also brought religion into the courtroom. For instance, Michael Capterton, a District Judge from Kentucky, has offered defendants charged with drug offenses a creative way of avoiding jail and confinement to treatment centers (Maimon, 2005). The judge allows them to attend worship services of their choice in lieu of more traditional sentences. He recently offered one offender the choice of 10 days in jail, a stay in rehabilitation center, or attendance at 10 worship services. While some critics have stated that the judge's sentences violate the separation of church and state, the judge indicates that going to services is not a requirement, and offenders can choose any religion they prefer. While the effects of the unconventional sentence have not been studied empirically, the judge feels that sentencing defendants to church has the potential to change lives.

Judges are also faced with religious appeals from attorneys and defendants. In *People v. Morgan* (1999), the defense attorney appealed to the judge's sense of religion by declaring "What I can bring forth before this court, at this time, is the knowledge and wisdom of Catholicism, the Pope, the archbishops." He further stated that the state "is proposing…that this court shall act in the stead of a God, that this court, with its supervising powers, shall become the almighty and terminate a man's life (p. 560)." Clearly, the attorney was using religion to persuade the judge.

Judges make decisions about cases that involve religion as well. For instance, the Supreme Court recently ruled that William Payton would not get a new trial even though the prosecutor had improperly discouraged the jury from adequately considering Payton's religious conversion (*Brown v. Payton*, 2005). The majority held that, even though the prosecutor had misinformed the jury about the relevance of the defendant's religious conversion, this misinformation would not have impacted the jurors' ultimate verdict. Judges have also had to rule on whether or not religion is an appropriate reason to exclude a juror during vior dire (e.g., *State v. Fuller*, 2004) and whether jurors can rely on Biblical guidance in their deliberations (*Colorado v. Harlan*, 2005). These examples indicate that judges' decisions about these religious issues can have a major impact on the trial process and outcomes.

Additionally, judges are faced with decisions in cases that have strong religious undertones, such as the right to hasten death, abortion, and homosexuality. Other judicial decisions involve whether schools can teach evolution or allow students to say the pledge of allegiance, whether the Ten Commandments can be displayed on government property and whether the government can issue school vouchers that allow students to attend private (usually religious) schools. Perhaps the most challenging issues courts have dealt with relate to marriage, because such cases are fraught with religious undertones. Religion and marriage have been entwined throughout history. In fact, marriage was governed by the Church throughout the Middle ages and by the ecclesiastical courts until the nineteenth-century (Reid, 2004).

Judges may rely on their own religious beliefs in such hard cases. Because the Establishment Clause prohibits judges, as state actors, from relying on religious justifications, opinions in such cases are often incomplete (Modak-Truran, 2004). Simply put, judges cannot admit that they issued an opinion based on religious reasoning, therefore they issue opinions with little reasoning. Thus, cases with inherently religious undertones are often underjustified, making case law in these areas unclear and ambiguous.

Still, some judges do outwardly rely on Biblical texts. In determining the legality of an anti-sodomy law, Justice Blackman (dissenting) indicated that such a law was not justified "beyond its conformity to religious doctrine." On the other hand, Chief Justice Burger (concurring) stated that the law was acceptable because it was "firmly rooted in Judaeo-Christian moral and ethical standards." (*Bowers v. Hardwick*, p. 196). The majority avoided religious reasoning, but determined that the prohibition against sodomy was based on "ancient roots" and thus was appropriate (*Bowers v. Hardwick*, 1986).

In another obvious reliance on Biblical instruction, the judge in *State v. Arnett* (2000) gave the defendant, who was convicted of raping a child, a lengthier sentence because of the judge's belief that the Bible supported severe sentences for those who injure children. The judge quoted the Bible in her words to the defendant, "Recently, Mr. Arnett, I had a murder case of an individual who had no remorse and the sentence was 20 years, and I thought about that in regards to sentencing you. Because I was looking for a source, what do I turn to, . . . to make that determination, what sentence you should get. . . . I finally answered my question late at night when I turned to one additional source to help me. . . . And that passage where I had the opportunity to look is Matthew 18:5, 6. "And whoso shall receive one such little child in my name, (sic) received me. But, (sic) whoso shall offend one of these little ones which believe in me, it were better for him that a millstone were hanged about his neck, and that (sic) he were drowned in the depth of the sea (p. 795)." The judge concluded with, "Mr. Arnett, I hope God has mercy on you and the hell that you have created. Thank you. (p. 795-6)." More recently, the judge in *State v. Holmes* (2005) stated that he prays that the sentence would be "adequate * * * for your soul" (p. 565).

Courts have had to determine whether judges have overstepped their boundaries by relying on the Bible. The Ohio Supreme Court determined that judges violate the defendants due process rights by relying on religious beliefs or tests. However such conduct is not completely impermissible if the judge adheres to the state's sentencing procedures and the religious appeals do not make the proceedings fundamentally unfair (*State v. Arnett*, 2000; *State v. Holmes*, 2005).

While various authors have addressed the issue of judges' religiosity from a legal standpoint (Berg & Ross,

1998; Collett, 2000; Conkle, 1998; Echols, 2005; Greenlee, 2000; Griffen, 1998; Hylton, 1998; Idleman, 1998; Sisk, Heise & Morriss, 2004), there is limited empirical research to explain the role of religion in judicial decision-making. Researchers have found that religion does have an impact on judicial decision-making. Sisk and colleagues (2004) conducted a study that revealed that religion (e.g., affiliation of the parties, the judge, and the community) was a strong predictor of judicial decisions. Meanwhile, Songer and Tabrizi (2000) conducted a study to determine whether judges' religiosity was related to their voting behavior. They found that judges who were more evangelical were significantly more likely to vote to uphold the death penalty than judges who were Protestant or Jewish.

At the heart of this debate is whether a judge should allow religion to influence his decisions (see generally, Sisk, et. al., 2004). Specifically, some authors discourage judges from basing decisions on religious convictions while others find such reliance proper (for review, see Sisk, et. al., 2004). For instance, Stephen Carter (1989) determined that judges could rely on their personal religious beliefs just as they can rely on other moral convictions. Greenlee (2000) also supports judges who use their religious beliefs as a guide, as long as the judge is also acting according to the norms of their office. Garvey and Coney (1998) suggest that Catholic judges face a conflict between their religious beliefs and their obligations to their profession. Such a conflict may force the judges to excuse themselves from hearing some cases.

Almost certainly, it is difficult for judges to ignore their own religiosity, especially when deciding cases with religious undertones, such those dealing with abortion, homosexuality, and school prayer. Fueled by findings that religion does in fact affect judicial decision, the debate is likely to continue.

## OTHER EXAMPLES OF RELIGION IN THE LEGAL SYSTEM

Religion has also found its way into other areas of the legal system, such as those listed below.

• Some restorative justice programs encourage criminals to contact their victims and families and apologize. Such a measure is believed to help both the victim and defendant heal. Such letters could contain religious undertones. For example, a defendant who finds God while imprisoned may feel the need to confess and profess his newly found religious beliefs. Because such a letter could be used against the defendant at trial, the justice system effectively discourages religious redemption through these communications (see, e.g., Bader, 2003).

• Recently, some authors have been concerned that the precinct where people vote can affect their voting decisions. Specifically, if a person votes in a church, they may be more inclined to vote more conservatively than if they had voted in a non-religious setting (Glasgow, & Rutchick, 2005). Thus, religious voting sites have the potential to affect the laws that are enacted.

• A Colorado County Treasurer distributed booklets to jurors that instructed them to consult religious teachings when making their verdicts. The booklet also suggested that jurors should ignore the law or judicial instruction if it conflicts with religious instruction (Able, 2003). Such advice coming from a government authority could influence jurors to rely on religion in their decisions.

• There has been some concern recently about the growing number of prisoners following Islamic religions (Menon, 2004; Gorman, 2004; Seper, 2004; Smith, 2004; Zoll, 2005). Because these religions are sometimes associated with terrorism, authorities are concerned. A shortage of Muslim chaplains in prisons complicates the picture. Justice Department Inspector General Glenn A. Fine is concerned that inmates who are not guided by a traditional chaplain will be more likely to follow an extremist chaplain or develop distorted, extremist beliefs (Seper, 2004). However because prisoners do not give up their rights to practice religion when they are convicted, this issue has created much legal discussion (e.g., Menon, 2004; Gorman, 2004; Seper, 2004; Smith, 2004; Zoll, 2005).

• Government agencies have issued reports concerning new religious movements in an attempt to influence policy (Richardson & Introvigne, 2001). Such reports raise concerns that new religious groups practice brainwashing or mind control, although such notions have largely been discounted through recent scholarship (Richardson & Introvigne, 2001). Although the idea that new religious movements brainwash their members began as an American phenomenon, it has caught on across Europe as well. Such notions thus influence policymaking and serve to limit religious freedoms and create a moral panic in society. As noted by Richardson and Introvigne (2001), politicians may adopt these notions to appear to be defending the integrity of society by quashing such deviant religions.

• There is currently some controversy in North Carolina about the legality of using non-Christian religious texts for use in the swearing in process (Associated Press, July 27, 2005). Muslims from the Al-Ummil Ummat Islamic Center in Greensboro, North Carolina donated copies of the Quran to the local courthouse. However two judges decided that it was not legal to allow Muslims to take the oath on the Quran instead of the Bible. The American Civil Liberties Union filed a lawsuit against the case, arguing that such a policy unconstitutionally favors Christianity over other religions (Associated Press, July 27, 2005). The case was still pending at the time of this writing.

• A State Governor is one of the last legal actors that can affect whether a defendant is put to death. Even if a jury and appellate judges have all found that the defendant received a proper trial, is guilty, and should be put to death, a governor can issue a pardon to spare the defendant's life. Such was the case when Illinois Governor George Ryan commuted the sentences of all 167 death row inmates in the state (Flock, 2003). More recently, Virginia's Governor Mark Warner spared the life of a convicted killer (CNN.com, November 29, 2005). Although governors are unlikely to publicly admit that their religious beliefs towards the death penalty drove a decision to pardon a death row inmate, it is possible that such beliefs play at least a small role in the decision.

    • Even the President has the potential to allow religion into the legal system. When President George W. Bush nominated Harriet Miers for Supreme Court, he said that his nomination was partially based on her evangelical Christian beliefs, stating "Part of Harriet Miers' life is her religion (CNN.com, October 12, 2005)." The President's nomination of a religious individual to the Supreme Court has the potential to affect the laws of the country if that justice allows her religiosity to affect her decisions.

CONCLUSION

The use of religion in the legal system is certainly a controversial topic. Some authors contend that reliance on religious teachings threatens the separation of church and state and violates the First Amendment's Establishment Clause (Egland, 2004; Simson & Garvey, 2001). Simson and Garvey (2001) argue that religion should be eliminated in all aspects of a trial because any reliance on religion is a violation of the Clause. Because judges and prosecutors are state actors, any religious references could arguably be seen as a violation of the Establishment Clause. Likewise, defense attorneys, while not state actors, could be seen as such by jurors. Simson and Garvey (2001) further argue that jurors also are considered actors of the state for Establishment Clause purposes, thus they should not rely on religion in their verdicts.

While most courts do not take such a strict stand about the use of religion as do Simson and Garvey, a few have recognized potential negative effects. For instance, some courts have determined that the use of religious arguments by attorneys violate the defendant's due process rights (e.g., *Boyd v. French*, 1998; *State v. Haselden*, 2003), or violate the Eighth Amendment (e.g., *Carruthers v. State*, 2000).

As this chapter demonstrated, there are many ways religion can infiltrate the legal system. Religion can affect every stage of a criminal trial, beginning with jury selection and ending with the Governor's pardon decision. Religion can also affect other aspects of the legal system, such as policymaking, judicial appointments, and voting behavior. Although there are many ways religion can affect the legal system, this book will focus primarily on religious appeals used in attorneys' closing arguments.

# CHAPTER 4

# Common Prosecution Appeals

In a courtroom, a jury hears a prosecutor's closing argument in a capital sentencing trial. The prosecutor stands before them, giving them instructions on how to make the life and death decision, "I want to quote a few things to you... in the book of Exodus... it says: He that smiteth a man, so that he die, shall be surely put to death.... And in Numbers, chapter 35, verse 18, it states: Or if he smite him with a hand weapon of wood, wherewith he may die, and he die, he is a murderer: the murderer shall surely be put to death... Whoever killeth any person, the murderer shall be put to death by the mouth of the witnesses. And moreover, you shall take no satisfaction for the life of a murderer which he is guilty of death but he shall surely be put to death. Ladies and gentlemen... That's what this Bible--what this good book says (*State v. Williams*, 1999, p. 642-3)." This was the religious appeal used in the case of *State v. Williams* (1999). Clearly, the prosecutor was appealing to the juror's sense of religiosity in order to secure a death penalty.

While it is difficult to know exactly how often such religious arguments are used, the increasing number of court decisions regarding appeals indicates that there may be a trend to use appeals more frequently. Accordingly, legal scholars have given the topic more attention in recent years (Blume & Johnson, 2000; Brooks, 1999; Duffy, 1997; Henson, 2001; Loewy, 2000; Miller & Bornstein,

2005; Simons, 2004; Simons, 2004; Simson & Garvey 2001;Walker, 2003).

Religious appeals used in closing arguments come in many forms, ranging from simple one-line Biblical quotes to detailed Biblical accounts of capital punishment. Three general categories of prosecutorial arguments have been used. First, attorneys have quoted Biblical passages that support retribution (*Green v. State*, 1996; *State v. Williams*, 1999). Second, prosecutors have claimed that God has given the state or the jurors authority to make the life and death decision, implying that God supports, or at least does not object to, the death penalty (*Coe v. Bell*, 1998; *State v. Middlebrooks*, 1999). Finally, prosecutors have made comparisons between the defendant and Biblical characters (e.g., the devil; *Commonwealth v. Henry*, 1990; *Cunningham v. Zant*, 1991) or between the defendant's crime and crimes committed in the Bible (e.g., Cain killing Abel; *Bussard v. Lockhart*, 1994; *People v. Jackson*, 1996; *State v. Holden*, 1997). Such appeals are designed to persuade the jury to side with the prosecution.

## RETRIBUTIVE COMMANDS

An example of a common retributive command used by prosecutors is the "eye for an eye" argument. (*Greene v. State*, 1996; *Hammond v. State*, 1995; *People v. Wash*, 1993; *State v. Shurn*, 1993; *Thompson v. State*, 1991). Such religious principles as "an eye for an eye" have been used in numerous societies for centuries (Simmonds, 2004). This doctrine describes the theory of retribution that many punitive systems are founded upon. Thus, it is not surprising that these appeals have found their way into the modern legal system.

Mosaic law that seemingly requires capital punishment for murder can be interpreted to mean that if someone (i.e., the defendant) kills someone, he too should be killed. Other popular appeals include versions of the quote "He that smiteth a man, so that he die, shall surely be put to death," (Exodus 21:12 King James Version; *People v. Mahaffey*, 1995; *People v. Wash*, 1993; *State v. Williams*, 1999), "whoso sheddeth man's blood, by man shall his blood be shed," (Genesis 9:6; *Carruthers v. State*, 2000; *Coe v. Bell*, 1998; *Doss v. State*, 1996; *Hammond v. State*, 1995; *State v. Middlebrooks*, 1999), or "the murderer shall surely be put to death" (Numbers 35:16; *State v. Daniels*, 1994; *Commonwealth v. Chambers*, 1991; *State v. Williams*, 1999). In a few cases, the prosecutor cited the commandment "thou shalt not kill" (Exodus, 20:13; *People v. Eckles*, 1980; *Robinson v. State*, 1995), combined with an explanation of how that directive applies to the defendant, but not to the state (*Bennett v. Angelone*, 1996; *Bracy v. Gramley*, 1996; *People v. Wash*, 1993). Such quotes are used by prosecutors to suggest that the defendant should be put to death and that the Bible supports, or even requires, such an outcome.

## CLAIMS OF DIVINE AUTHORITY

Another approach taken by prosecutors is to address the authority of the state or jury to put a defendant to death. Some lawyers have simply informed the jury that the judicial process does not surpass God's authority because the Bible allows the penalty (*Coe v. Bell*, 1998; *People v. Davenport*, 1996), while others have gone further by claiming that either the state legislature, the prosecutor, or the jury is acting under God's authority (*Bennett v. Angelone*, 1996; *Buttrum v. Black*, 1989; *Ex parte Waldrop*, 1984; *McNair v. State*, 1992; *People v. Rohn*, 1980; *State v. Moose*, 1984). One prosecutor claimed to be "the servant of God to execute His wrath on the wrongdoer" (*Buttrum v. Black*, 1989, p. 1316). Other attorneys have addressed the jury's authority to put the defendant to death. One attorney called the jury the "tool of the Lord," insinuating that God had given jurors the authority to make such decisions (*State v. Middlebrooks*, 1999, p. 559).

Another attorney pointed out that the Bible says, "Whosoever sheddeth man's blood, by man shall his blood be shed" and suggested that the jurors should be "true to

God" and make the proper sentence of death (*Coe v. Bell*, 1998, p. 330). Others have suggested that police and prosecutors are ordained to be representatives of God, and to disobey them is to resist God Himself. These attorneys bolster this argument by paraphrasing Romans 13:2, "whosoever therefore resisteth the power, resisteth the ordinance of God; and they that resist shall receive to themselves damnation" (e.g., *Miller v. North Carolina*, 1978; *Sandoval v. Calderon*, 2000, *State v. Moose*, 1984). Thus, these types of religious appeals are used to address jurors' concerns about the authority to make the life and death decision.

## COMPARISON TO BIBLICAL CHARACTERS OR METAPHORS

Attorneys' use of religious appeals is not limited to Biblical quotes; often, detailed metaphors are used to compare the defendant and crime to Biblical people and situations. Prosecutors have compared the defendant to infamous Biblical characters such as Judas Iscariot, (*Cunningham v. Zant*, 1991; *State v. Phillips*, 1997), false prophets (*State v. Lundgren*, 1995) and the devil or "Prince of Darkness" (*Commonwealth v. Henry*, 1990; *Commonwealth v. Whitney*, 1986; *State v. Cauthern*, 1996). Attorneys have also compared the crimes in question to the stories of Cain and Abel (*People v. Jackson*, 1996; *Shell v. State*, 1989; *State v. Alston*, 1995), David and Goliath (*State v. Gentry*, 1995), and the Apostle Peter (*U.S. v. Giry*, 1987).

Similarly, prosecutors have used Biblical metaphors to equate the defendant's situation to one in the Bible in which the wrongdoer received the penalty of death. In cases of child murder, prosecutors have paraphrased from Luke 17:2, "It were better for him that a millstone were hanged about his neck, and he cast into the sea, than that he should offend one of these little ones" to demonstrate that child murderers should receive the death penalty (e.g., *Commonwealth v. Brown*, 1998; *Long v. State*, 1972; *State v. Holden*, 1997; *State v. Sidden*, 1997).

Although religious appeals are used less frequently in the guilt phase (*Bussard v. Lockhart*, 1994; *State v. Lundgren*, 1995), the prosecutor in one notable case used a religious appeal in arguing that the defendant's behavior was proof of his guilt (*Bussard v. Lockhart*, 1994). The defendant had escaped from police and had avoided being apprehended for four years before being caught. At trial, the prosecuting attorney quoted a Biblical passage: "Proverbs 28:1 fits…just as clear as it can be, 'the guilty flee when no man pursueth while the righteous stand bold as a lion'…[defendant] fled to avoid coming to trial; that shows guilt (p. 324)." When used in this manner, metaphors and comparisons to Biblical characters both suggest to the jury that the Bible recommends the death penalty for individuals such as the defendant.

## MISCELLANEOUS PROSECUTION ARGUMENTS

Other religious appeals made by prosecutors do not seem to fit clearly into any of the categories discussed above. For instance, prosecutors have hypothesized that execution might be the only way the defendant could receive salvation (*People v. Wrest*, 1992; *Sandoval v. Calderon*, 2000), and have questioned the sincerity of the defendant's religious beliefs or religious conversion (*Commonwealth v. Cook*, 1996; *People v. Payton*, 1992). Other prosecutors have argued that the defendant did not allow the victim an opportunity to reconcile with God, or become all that God had planned (*Commonweath v. Brown*, 1998; *Eldred v. Commonwealth*, 1994). Attorneys have argued that, since the defendant was the son of a minister, he was bound more than most people by the Fifth commandment "thou shalt not kill," indicating that the jurors should hold the defendant to a higher standard of behavior than the average citizen (*People v. Eckles*, 1980; *State v. Wangberg*, 1965). One attorney questioned whether God recognizes the insanity defense as an excuse for killing, suggesting that the jurors find him guilty even if he was legally insane (*State v.*

*Wangberg*, 1965).  Such arguments rely less on convincing the jurors that the Bible supports the death sentence and instead relies more on arousing jurors' emotions and altering their opinions of the defendant.

CONCLUSION

In their attempts to convince a jury to decide on a death sentence, prosecuting attorneys use a variety of persuasive tactics.  Religious appeals are one such tactic that could be persuasive to jurors.  Religious appeals remind jurors that God has commanded "thou shalt not kill" and "the murderer shall be put to death."  While some jurors, such as those who do not believe in God, will not be persuaded by such arguments, other jurors are likely to be swayed.

# CHAPTER 5

# Common Defense Appeals

Chapter Four presented a host of religious appeals that have been used by the prosecutor to try to convince a jury to give the death penalty. Religious appeals have also been used by defense attorneys, who indicate that the Bible calls for mercy and not retribution or revenge. Defense appeals are harder to research than prosecution appeals, however. Religious appeals used by defense attorneys rarely appear in appellate cases since the Double Jeopardy clause of the Fifth Amendment prevents defendants from being retried after acquittal. Accordingly, if the defendant is successful, the case never reaches the appeals court. Defense arguments are discussed, however, in appellate cases in which the defense attorneys were precluded from making religious arguments, in appeals for ineffective counsel, and in cases where both the prosecution and defense attorneys used religious appeals. While defense arguments that incorporate religious appeals are found infrequently in appeals court cases, there are enough to determine several distinct types of appeals.

Commonly, defense appeals take the form of Biblical commands that forbid execution or promote mercy (*Bennett v. Angelone*, 1996; *State v. Messiah*, 1988). Other attorneys have offered Biblical stories that promote mercy (*Bennett v. Angelone*, 1996; *State v. Patterson*, 1996; *State v. Shafer*, 2000). Less frequently, attorneys offer general quotes about judging others or claim that religious authorities are opposed to the death penalty (*People v. Freeman*, 1994; *People v. Wash*, 1993).

## BIBLICAL COMMANDS AGAINST EXECUTION

Just as prosecutors cite Biblical passages that seemingly approve of the death penalty, defense attorneys cite passages that allegedly forbid it. For example, attorneys commonly quote such passages as "Vengeance is mine, thus sayeth the Lord," or argue generally that life and death decisions belong to God, not to man (e.g., *Bennett v. Angelone*, 1996; *State v. Middlebrooks*, 1999). Another common tactic is to directly attack the prosecution's use of the "eye for an eye" argument by presenting the following quote from Jesus: "You have heard that it has been said 'an eye for an eye and a tooth for a tooth;' but I say to you, do not resist an evil doer. But if someone strikes you on the right cheek, turn the other also" (Matthew 5:38-39). Attorneys using this "turn the other cheek" argument insinuate that the prosecution's "eye for an eye" argument is not valid because of the later teachings of Jesus (e.g., *Bennett v. Angelone*, 1996; *State v. Messiah*, 1988). Such appeals suggest to the jury that the Bible forbids the death penalty, thus the defendant should receive a lesser sentence.

## BIBLICAL STORIES PROMOTING MERCY

Defense attorneys also appeal to the jury's sense of compassion by giving specific examples of mercy in the Bible. One such argument is adapted from the story told in the book of John, Chapter 8, in which a woman is caught in the act of adultery. Jesus tells her would-be executioners, "He that is without sin among you, let him cast the first stone," suggesting that as all are guilty of bad acts, man should not punish his fellow man. Later in the story, Jesus released the woman stating, "Neither do I condemn you, go and do not sin again." The implication is that Jesus stopped the execution in favor of mercy and forgiveness, thus jurors should do the same (e.g., *State v. Patterson*, 1996[3]; *State v. Shafer*, 2000).

This "casting stones" argument was used in the sentencing phase of the trial of Susan Smith, a woman who claimed that a carjacker had stolen her car with her two children inside, later to confess that she had killed her sons herself and had told police the carjacking story to cover up the crime (Burritt, 1995). Smith's attorney picked up the clerk of court's Bible and told the story of the adulterous woman, telling jurors "He who is without sin among you, let him first cast a stone... You each have a stone, with 12 in all... but no stone may be thrown unless all are thrown" (Burritt, 1995). Although no one can know if these arguments affected the jurors' decision-making, the jury returned a sentence of life imprisonment despite a strong public sentiment that Smith should receive the death penalty (Morganthau, 1995).

Defense attorneys also recount the story of the crucifixion of Jesus, and point out that Jesus said from the cross, "Forgive them for they know not what they do," instead of asking God to condemn the men to death (Luke 23:34; e.g., *Bennett v. Angleone*, 1996; *State v. Messiah*, 1988). Other lawyers have told the story of Cain and Abel, noting that Cain was not put to death for killing his brother (*Commonwealth v. Daniels*, 1994; *People v. Bradford*, 1997). Such examples suggest to the jury that they should exercise mercy as God did in these examples.

## MISCELLANEOUS DEFENSE ARGUMENTS

Some defense attorneys make general claims that most religions and religious leaders oppose the death penalty (*People v. Wash*, 1993), or that some interpretations of the Bible suggest that God is against the death penalty (*People v. Wash*, 1993; *Sandoval v. Calderon*, 2000). One defense

---

[3] Although the attorney planned on telling this Biblical story, the judge prohibited such argument, and the appeals court affirmed the decision.

attorney even went so far as to say that the death penalty is against Christian beliefs and that jurors who impose it will suffer after death (*McNair v. State*, 1992).

Other appeals target the jurors' sense of personal responsibility or morality. Attorneys have made statements such as "love your neighbor as yourself" (e.g., *State v. Daniels*, 1994) and "Judge not that ye be not judged" (*People v. Freeman*, 1994) to encourage jurors to spare their clients. Others have told the jurors that they are "playing God" if they choose vengeance (*Sandoval v. Calderon*, 2000). Finally, some defendants offer religious arguments as evidence of their good moral character, indicating that the defendant is or has become a religious believer who is not deserving of death (*Commonwealth v. Cook*, 1996; *Ice v. Commonwealth*, 1984; *People v. Clark*, 1993; *People v. Payton*, 1992; *Robinson v. State*, 1995).

CONCLUSION

While less frequent than prosecution appeals, defense appeals are sometimes used to persuade jurors to have mercy on the defendant. These defense appeals come in many forms, but all are intended to remind jurors that God allows forgiveness and encourages compassion. Defense appeals, just like prosecution appeals, are likely to be more persuasive to those who believe in God and the Bible. Even if such appeals are only influential to a small number of jurors, these appeals have the potential to have a major impact on death penalty trials. While prosecutors have to convince all 12 jurors in order to secure a death penalty, the defense attorney needs to convince only one juror to essentially protect his client's life. If at least one juror refuses to give the death penalty, the jury will be unable to reach unanimity and will be a "hung jury." In the event of a hung jury, the defendant will receive a sentence of life in prison, unless the judge orders a new trial. Thus, defense appeals have the potential to save a defendant's life.

# CHAPTER 6

# Court Decisions Regarding Religion in Closing Arguments

With the wealth of both prosecution and defense appeals, it is no surprise that courts have had to make important decisions regarding the use of appeals. Courts are far from agreement about the permissibility of such appeals. Some courts prohibit all appeals (*Commonwealth v. Chambers*, 1991; *Commonwealth v. Cook*, 1996; *Commonwealth v. Daniels*, 1994) while others have announced that they are generally permissible (*State v. Artis*, 1989; *State v. Daniels*, 1994; *State v. Fullwood*, 1988; *State v. Holden*, 1997; *State v. Williams*, 1999;).

Still other courts have allowed some types of appeals, yet restricted the use of others (*Commonwealth v. Daniels*, 1994; *Cunningham v. Zant*, 1991; *Greene v. State*, 1996; *Hill v. State*, 1993; *State v. Cauthern*, 1996; *State v. Debler*, 1993; *State v. Gibbs*, 1993; *State v. Phillips*, 1997). Others have advised attorneys to refrain from using appeals, but did not specifically rule on their permissibility (*People v. Pizzaro*, 2004; *People v. Woolley*, 2002). In certain circumstances, courts have affirmed convictions despite improper arguments by prosecutors, calling the improper arguments "harmless" error (*Bennett v. Angelone*, 1996; *Gibson v. State*, 1972; *People v. Eckles*, 1980; *People v. Wash*, 1993; *People v. Wrest*, 1992) or declaring them a fair response to defendant's religious evidence or arguments (*Boyd v. French*, 1998; *Commonwealth v. Cook*,

1996; *Commonwealth v. Whitney*, 1986; *Crowe v. State*, 1995; *McNair v. State*, 1997; *People v. Hill*, 1992; *People v. Mahaffey*, 1995; *Shell v. State*, 1989; *Thompson v. State*, 1991).

Often, courts have affirmed because the trial court had issued a curative instruction (*Boyd v. French*, 1998; *People v. Davenport*, 1996; *People v. Mahaffey*, 1995; *People v. Wash*, 1993; *State v. Williams*, 1997; *United States. v. Giry*, 1987). Rules governing the use of religious appeals have been issued by both state courts and federal courts, and have been suggested by authors of various law review articles (Blume and Johnson, 2000; Brooks, 1999; Duffy, 1997; Simson & Garvey, 2001). Each judicial rule is described below, followed by a summary of the reasons courts have found religious appeals legally impermissible.

## RULES REGULATING RELIGIOUS APPEALS

### All References Prohibited

Two state courts (Pennsylvania and Tennessee) and two federal circuits (Fourth and Ninth Circuits) have adopted the most restrictive approaches to religious arguments (e.g., *Boyd v. French*, 1998; *Commonwealth v. Chambers*, 1991; *Commonwealth v. DeJesus*, 2004; *Sandoval v. Calderon*, 2001; *State v. Middlebrooks*, 1999). The Pennsylvania Supreme Court held that "reliance in any manner upon the Bible or any other religious writing in support of the imposition of a penalty of death is reversible error per se and may subject violators to disciplinary action (*Commonwealth v. Chambers*, 1991, p. 644)." This holding was later extended to religious arguments made by defense counsel (*Commonwealth v. Daniels*, 1994) and limited to Biblical appeals that were made specifically to support or oppose the death penalty (*Commonwealth v. Cook*, 1996). While all appeals are forbidden, the Pennsylvania court has made it clear that the attorney's statements must be clearly Biblical. If the statement is not "distinctively" Biblical (*Commonwealth v. Spotz*, 2000), it will be allowed.

Although the rule in Tennessee does not require automatic reversal of the sentence, the Tennessee courts have declared impermissible all references to Biblical passages, religious law, paraphrases of Biblical passages, and comparisons to Biblical figures (*State v. Middlebrooks*, 1999). However, if appeals are used, the defendant's sentence is not automatically reversed; the case must pass the harmless error test before being remanded for resentencing (*State v. Richardson*, 1998). For example, the court in *State v. Richardson* recognized that the state prohibits all Biblical appeals, yet the court determined that the error would not have affected the outcome of the case. The Tennessee prohibition rule has proved to be all talk and no action, as no case has yet to be overturned solely on the grounds of religious appeals, although the court has had several opportunities to do so (*State v. Cauthern*, 1996; *State v. Cribbs*, 1998; *State v. Middlebrooks*, 1999; *State v. Richardson*, 1998).

The Fourth Circuit has declared that Biblical appeals are "undoubtedly . . .improper (*Boyd v. French*, 1998, p. 329)," "universally condemned (*Bennett v. Angelone*, 1996, p. 1346)" and "have no place in our non-ecclesiastical courts and may not be tolerated (*Bennett v. Angelone*, 1996, p. 1346)." Similarly, the Ninth Circuit held that it is inappropriate to present the jury with Biblical law for consideration in the sentencing determination (*Sandoval v. Calderon*, 2001). These four jurisdictions have adopted the most restrictive policies toward religious appeals as they have found such appeals generally improper.

## References are Generally Permissible

While some courts have generally forbidden Biblical appeals (*Commonwealth v. Brown*, 1998; *Commonwealth v. Chambers*, 1991; *State v. Middlebrooks*, 1999), other courts have found that such arguments are generally permissible (*State v. Daniels*, 1994; *State v. Williams*, 1999). These courts have found that it was not "so grossly improper" to argue that the Bible does not prohibit the death penalty (*State v. Williams*, 1999, p. 642), that such arguments generally fall within proper grounds allowed in highly contested cases (*State v. Artis*, 1989; *State v. Daniels*, 1994; *State v. Fullwood*, 1988; *State v. Holden*, 1997), are within the scope of an attorney's poetic license (*Bussard v. Lockhard*, 1994; *Commonwealth v. Henry*, 1990; *Commonwealth v. Whitney*, 1986) or are an appropriate account of the history of the death penalty (*Berry v. State*, 1997; *State v. Williams*, 1999). Thus, many courts have determined that religious appeals are appropriate references for use in closing arguments.

Wide Latitude

While some courts have forbidden appeals and others have found them permissible, most courts fall somewhere in between these extremes. Moderate courts allow attorneys wide latitude in using appeals (*Berry v. State*, 1997; *Cole v. State*, 2003; *State v. Gibbs*, 1993) but suggest general guidelines. For example, courts have determined that appeals are acceptable as long as they are not excessive (*Christenson v. State*, 2004; *State v. Debler*, 1993; *State v. Phillips*, 1997), are not grossly improper (*State v. Haselden*, 2003; State v. Williams, 1999); do not go beyond the character of the defendant or the circumstances of the case (*Commonwealth v. Daniels*, 1994; *State v. Cauthern*, 1996), or do not inflame the passions or prejudice of the jurors (*Cunningham v. Zant*, 1991). For instance, the court in *Christenson v. State* (2004) determined that the appeal was not an error because it was isolated and was not excessive.

Other courts have held that appeals are permissible as long as they do not argue that the death penalty should be based on the defendant's religious beliefs (*Greene v. State*, 1996; *Hill v. State*, 1993), do not argue that Biblical law requires a certain verdict or sentence (*Commonwealth v. Brown*, 1998; *Commonweath v. Chambers*, 1991; *People v. Harrison*, 2005) or are not so improper that they prevent a fair trial (*State v. Ramsey*, 1993). One court determined that an appeal was appropriate because "rather than invoking religious law over secular law, this argument merely urges jurors to make the decision the State viewed as the proper one--recommending a death sentence (*State v. Roache*, 2004, p. 431)." Thus, the court suggests that appeals are acceptable as long as they do not promote Biblical law over the law of the state.

A similar wide latitude rule is the distinction between improper commanding and proper explanatory appeals. Several Georgia cases demonstrate the distinction between religious arguments that are merely explanatory and religious arguments that are commanding. In *Christenson v. State* (1991), the court found a religious reference acceptable because it merely used a Biblical reference to explain the concept of retribution. On the other hand, in *Hammond v. State* (1995), the court drew a line between such explanatory references and references that were more direct or commanding in nature. The court determined that more direct religious appeals were impermissible because they implied that the Bible required the death penalty, and thus violated the defendant's rights by encouraging the death penalty for all homicides without regard to aggravating or mitigating circumstances. Ultimately, the Georgia courts have allowed brief, explanatory religious appeals, but indicated that commanding references to Biblical commands are improper. California has also adopted such a rule, determining that prosecutors can use religious appeals as long as they do not appeal to religious authority or argue that Biblical law requires a certain outcome (*People v. Harrison*, 2005).

In *Sandoval v. Calderon* (2000), the Ninth Circuit Court of Appeals adopted a similar distinction between commanding and explanatory appeals. The court found that the defense use of the phrase "playing God" and the reference to "an eye for an eye" to be acceptable because the phrases were used in a secular argument critical of vengeance. Since the defense did not claim that the Bible required a certain sentence (i.e., life in prison), it was ruled proper. On the other hand, the prosecutor used Biblical appeals that were "eloquent, powerful, and unmistakably Biblical in style (*Sandoval v. Calderon*, 2000, p. 778)" The prosecutor inferred that the state was empowered with authority by God to punish wrong-doers, like the defendant. Further, if the jurors did not obey authority (i.e., by giving the death penalty), God would punish them. The court summarized the Biblical appeals by stating, "There could be no clearer an invocation of divine authority to direct a jury's verdict (p. 779)." Thus the court determined that these Biblical appeals prejudiced the defendant because they commanded a certain sentence (i.e., death penalty). These courts have determined that commanding appeals (e.g., that the Bible requires a certain sentence) are influential enough to improperly sway jurors while explanatory appeals (e.g., using Biblical examples of vengeance and retribution) are not.

Fair Response Rule

Often, the prosecutor is allowed to use religious arguments if the defendant has first offered religious appeals or evidence (*Boyd v. French*, 1998; *Commonwealth v. Cook*, 1996; *Commonwealth v. Whitney*, 1986; *Crowe v. State*, 1995; *McNair v. State*, 1997; *People v. Hill*, 1992; *People v. Mahaffey*, 1995; *Shell v. State*, 1989; *State v. Murphy*, 2001; *State v. Roache*, 2004; *Thompson v. State*, 1991). For instance, the defense attorney in *State v. Murphy* (2001) told the jurors "[W]e are taught in our Sunday schools that mercy is good [and] that we may hate the sin but care for the sinner… Spare the life of Ulysses Murphy, and you, too… will be blessed (p. 796)." The prosecutor responded by telling the jurors that the defendant "will have to ask God for" mercy (p. 796). The defense attorney appealed the sentence, stating that the prosecutor's comment was an improper religious appeal. The court determined that the prosecutor's argument was proper because it was a fair response to the defense attorney's own religious appeal (*State v. Murphy*, 2001).

In general, courts have determined that prosecutors are allowed more leeway in rebuttal, and in some circumstances, may be allowed to make arguments that would be otherwise impermissible (*Sandoval v. Calderon*, 2000; *State v. Ramsey*, 1993). For example, some courts have allowed religious arguments because the appeal was offered as a legitimate response to the defense counsel's mitigating evidence concerning the defendant's religious activities (*Crowe v. State*, 1995; *Commonwealth v. Cook*, 1996).

Courts that allow religious appeals by the prosecution in rebuttal believe that the "prosecutor's brief comments were invited by, and made insignificant by . . . references made by the defendant (*People v. Mahaffey*, 1995, p. 1069)." It is not clear, however, whether or not use of religious appeals by the prosecution actually is made insignificant simply because the defense made opposing religious appeals. It is possible that references made by the prosecutor may be more persuasive than those of the defense, thus still affecting the jurors. For example, the defense may call a pastor as a witness to testify about the defendant's religiosity, prompting the prosecutor to cite Biblical passages requiring the death penalty. If the prosecutor's arguments are stronger than the pastor's testimony, the final outcome is detrimental to the defendant. This possibility is reflected in two notable cases (*Commonwealth v. Brown*, 1998; *State v. Middlebrooks*, 1999).

In these cases, the court determined that the prosecutor's use of religious appeals was "not justifiable pursuant to the doctrine of fair response (*Commonwealth v. Brown*, 1998, p. 494; see also *State v. Middlebrooks*, 1999)." Thus, the prosecutor is not allowed total freedom to use religious appeals just because the defendant has done so first. Such a decision may reflect the courts' recognition that appeals by the defense may not offset appeals by the prosecution, creating an inequity of arguments and potentially violating the defendant's rights.

## Harmless Error Rule

Many courts have found that the religious appeals were prejudicial or violated the defendant's rights, yet ultimately determined that these remarks were harmless error (*Bennett v. Angelone*, 1996; *Boyd v. French*, 1998; *Cole v. State*, 2003; *Gibson v. State*, 1972; *Hammond v. State*, 1995; *People v. Eckles*, 1980; *People v. Pizzaro*, 2004; *People v. Wash*, 1993, *People v. Wrest*, 1992; *State v. Cauthern*, 1996; *State v. Hatcher*, 2004). For instance, the court in *State v. McCary* (2003) found the religious appeals were inflammatory and improper, but not so much that they affected the ultimate verdict. Such findings are usually based on the determination that the remarks were too brief to be influential to the jury (*People v. Eckles*, 1980; *People v. Pizzaro*, 2004; *People v. Wrest*, 1992) or too weak in light of the totality of the evidence (*Bennett v. Angelone*, 1996; *Crowe v. State*, 1995; *Gibson v. State*, 1972).

The court in *State v. Ceballos* (2003) developed a two-step progression to determine if a religious appeal was appropriate or unfair. First, the court determines whether the statements were inflammatory or prejudicial. If the statements are found to be improper, the court makes a determination that attorney "misconduct" has occurred. The second step determines whether the attorney's misconduct was substantial. That is, the defendant must show that the misconduct was so substantial that the entire trial was fundamentally unfair. If so, then the defendant was denied due process. If both requirements are not found to exist, then the court determines that the religious appeal was acceptable (*State v. Ceballos*, 2003).

When applying the harmless error rule, the court weighs all factors in the case and determines if the jury would have reached the same verdict even without the prejudicial remarks. For example, the court in *State v. Thompson* (2003) did not find that the religious appeal "viewed in the collective with other [improper] statements ... [was] substantially prejudicial such that the fundamental fairness of the trial was adversely impacted (p. 653)." The court typically considers the weight of the evidence, the probable impact on the jury, the deliberate nature of the conduct, the length of the trial, and the judge's curative instructions to determine whether the appeal was harmless error (see Duffy, 1997).

The Supreme Court has instructed appellate courts to apply the harmless error rule when reviewing cases and to ignore errors that the court finds harmless, even if the error was a violation of a constitutional right (*United States v. Hasting*, 1983; *Chapman v. California*, 1967). Using this procedure, some courts have declined to determine whether or not the remarks were prejudicial because "there is no reasonable probability that this argument, even if improper, changed the result of trial (*Crowe v. State*, 1995, p. 811)." Another court determined that, in a close case, use of improper Biblical arguments could "tip the balance, justifying a reversal (*Gibson v. State*, 1972, p. 900)," however since the weight of evidence in this particular case strongly supported the death sentence, it was deemed harmless.

One notable exception is the Georgia Supreme Court's declaration that the standard of review for such cases is not a matter of "whether the improper argument in reasonable probability changed the result of the trial, but simply whether the argument was objectionable and prejudicial (*Carruthers v. State*, 2000, p. 223)." The court in *State v. Richardson* also voiced its displeasure at the harmless error rule by stating that "[a]t some point, the need to preserve the integrity of the judicial process will require that the continued practice not be subject to the harmless error rule (*State v. Richardson*, 1998, p. 128)." These courts are a minority, as far more courts have adopted the harmless error rule and determined that improper remarks do not require reversal.

Curative Instruction

At times an appeals court will rule that an improper remark was harmless because the trial judge issued a curative instruction after the religious appeals were offered (*Boyd v. French*, 1998; *Lewis v. State*, 2004; *People v. Mahaffey*, 1995; *State v. Richardson*, 1998; *United States. v. Giry*, 1987). For instance, the court in *Lewis v. State* (2004) found the prosecutor's religious appeal improper but did not reverse the sentence. The trial court had issued a curative instruction ordering the jurors to disregard the appeal.

Similarly, courts have found religious appeals permissible if the attorney who makes the appeal ultimately tells the jury to follow state law (*People v. Davenport*, 1996; *People v. Wash*, 1993; *State v. Williams*, 1997). For example, the court allowed such statements as "God allowed men to carry out his word. God gave us Bibles . . . to follow and we as [a] society have decided through God that what we are doing is not wrong" in part because the prosecutor also stated that the "imposition of the death penalty was not usurping God's authority but legitimately carrying out California law (*People v. Davenport*, 1996, p. 1223)." These courts assume that the jury understood the judge's instructions and properly disregarded the improper religious appeal.

As this review demonstrates, there is much disagreement over the permissibility of religious appeals. Various courts have prohibited all appeals (*Commonwealth v. Chambers*, 1991; *Commonwealth v. Daniels*, 1994; *Commonwealth v. DeJesus*, 2004; *Commonwealth v. Cook*, 1996), found them generally permissible (*State v. Artis*, 1989; *State v. Daniels*, 1994; *State v. Fullwood*, 1988; *State v. Holden*, 1997; *State v. Williams*, 1999) advised attorneys to refrain from using appeals, (*People v. Pizzaro*, 2004; *People v. Woolley*, 2002), and have offered rules distinguishing rules that are permissible from those that are impermissible (*Cole v. State*, 2003; *Commonwealth v. Daniels*, 1994; *Cunningham v. Zant*, 1991; *Greene v. State*, 1996; *Hill v. State*, 1993; *State v. Cauthern*, 1996; *State v. Debler*, 1993; *State v. Gibbs*, 1993; *State v. Phillips*,1997).

Even when arguments are found to be improper, they have sometimes been allowed because they are found to be harmless error (*Bennett v. Angelone*, 1996; *Gibson v. State*,

1972; *People v. Eckles*, 1980; *People v. Pizzaro*, 2004; *People v. Wash*, 1993; *People v. Wrest*, 1992), because they were offered in fair response to defendant's religious evidence or arguments (*Boyd v. French*, 1998; *Commonwealth v. Cook*, 1996; *Crowe v. State*, 1995; *McNair v. State*, 1997; *People v. Hill*, 1992; *People v. Mahaffey*, 1995; *Shell v. State*, 1989; *State v. Roache*, 2004; *Thompson v. State*, 1991) or because the trial judge had issued a curative instruction (*Boyd v. French*, 1998; *Lewis v. State*, 2004; *People v. Davenport*, 1996; *People v. Mahaffey*, 1995; *People v. Wash*, 1993; *State v. Williams*, 1997; *United States. v. Giry*, 1987). Even though some courts have ruled that appeals are permissible or harmless, others have strongly disagreed. Several courts have determined that such appeals are impermissible for a variety of legal reasons.

## DECISIONS ABOUT THE LEGALITY OF RELIGIOUS APPEALS

When courts have found prosecution appeals to be impermissible, they often rule that such appeals are not allowed because they violate the defendant's constitutional rights. Defense attorney appeals have also been found to be legally impermissible, for example because they lead jurors to follow law other than that of the state. A review of these legal decisions reveals a number of legal bases for finding appeals impermissible.

### Legality of Prosecution Appeals

Convicted defendants generally challenge religious appeals because they feel that such appeals violate their right to due process (*Bennett v. Angelone*, 1996; *Boyd v. French*, 1998; *People v. Wash*, 1993; *State v. Haselden*, 2003), the Eighth Amendment (*Carruthers v. State*, 2000; *State v. Artis*, 1989), or the First Amendment separation of church and state (*People v. Wash*, 1993; *State v. Artis*, 1989). Courts have also found that such arguments are improper because they are inflammatory or improperly invoke the prejudice or passions of the jurors (*Cunningham v. Zant*, 1991; *U.S. v. Giry*, 1987).

Various courts have ruled that Biblical appeals violate the defendant's Eighth Amendment rights for either or both of two distinct reasons. First, several courts have held that religious appeals violate the requirement that states provide juries with "channeled discretion" in determining which defendants should or should not be put to death. Because "Biblical law" tends to contain "all or nothing" commands that do not allow jurors to consider whether this particular defendant deserves the penalty based on the unique facts of the case, they have been found improper (*Carruthers v. State*, 2000; *Sandoval v. Calderon*, 2000). Second, courts have found that religious appeals reduce the responsibility that jurors feel for making the sentencing decision (*People v. Wash*, 1993; *Sandoval v. Calderon*, 2000).

## The Requirement of Channeled Discretion

Under the Constitution, an individual who is accused of a crime is granted the right to be free from cruel and unusual punishment. In 1972, the Supreme Court in *Furman v. Georgia* (1972) determined that the death penalty violated the Eighth Amendment because it was administered in an arbitrary manner by allowing the jury "unbridled discretion" in sentencing. After the *Furman* decision, states adopted statutes that would help channel the jury's discretion in their sentencing decisions and provide further safeguards for defendants. In 1976, the Supreme Court in *Gregg v. Georgia* (1976) and its companion cases approved of new statutes that guided jurors by providing a limited number of bases upon which they could determine whether the defendant should receive the death penalty or a lesser sentence. For instance, one common statutory scheme requires that jurors weigh statutorily determined aggravating and mitigating factors in reaching their decision. Thus, a death penalty can only be imposed when jurors make their sentencing decision based on these specific factors as set forth by statute (*Godfrey v. Georgia*, 1980).

Courts have found that religious appeals violate this "channeled discretion" rule because many Biblical passages are blanket statements requiring (e.g., the "eye for an eye" argument) or forbidding (e.g., the "turn the other cheek" argument) the death penalty (*Carruthers v. State*, 2000; *Hammond v. State*, 1995; *Jones v. Kemp*, 1989; *Sandoval v. Calderon*, 2000). For instance, the *Hammond* court rejected a religious appeal that suggested that Biblical law required the death penalty for all homicides. The court stated that the appeal was a clear violation of a Georgia law requiring the jury to find at least one statutory aggravating factor in order to impose the death penalty.

Clearly, courts are concerned that religious arguments will lead individuals to rely on Biblical law instead of solely on state law (*Carruthers v. State*, 2000; *Commonwealth v. Chambers*, 1991; *Ice v. Commonwealth*, 1984; *Jones v. Kemp*, 1989; *People v. Wash*, 1993; *People v. Wrest*, 1992; *Sandoval v. Calderon*, 2000; *State v. Wangberg*, 1965). For instance, religious appeals may encourage jurors to impose a death sentence without regard to the evidence, simply because they feel that Biblical law requires the death sentence. The court in *Carruthers v. State* (2000) rejected the use of appeals such as "Whoever sheds another person's blood shall have his own blood shed by man" by stating, "in contrast to Biblical law, Georgia law gives the jury the discretion to recommend life imprisonment or death, provides stringent procedures and safeguards that must be followed during the trial, and permits the jury to impose the death penalty only in limited circumstances (p. 222)." In sum, various courts have determined that religious arguments are impermissible when they act to discourage jurors from following state law that channels their decision in ways required by the line of Supreme Court cases discussed above.

Relieving the Jury of Responsibility: The Caldwell Rule

The Supreme Court in *Caldwell v. Mississippi* (1985) determined that it is improper to lead a jury to believe that the responsibility for making the sentencing decision is not theirs alone. Simply put, the Eighth Amendment prohibits any argument that prevents a juror from recognizing the gravity of their decision. Several courts have determined that religious arguments improperly reduce the jurors' sense of responsibility (*Carruthers v. State*, 2000; *People v. Wash*, 1993; *People v. Wrest*, 1992; *Sandoval v. Calderon*, 2000). Such appeals are said to "minimize the jury's responsibility" and provide the jurors "an easy way to avoid a hard choice (*People v. Sandoval*, 1992, p. 890)." These courts are concerned that religious appeals may increase the likelihood of death sentences by allowing jurors to avoid any negative feelings associated with sentencing the defendant to death. Instead of taking personal responsibility, jurors can place the responsibility for the decision on God or on Biblical law, which could relieve any negative feelings.

The Inflammatory Nature of Religious Arguments

In addition to the Eighth Amendment violations listed above, religious appeals have been found improper because they inflame the passions and prejudices of the jurors (*Cunningham v. Zant*, 1991; *U.S. v. Giry*, 1987). Generally, prosecutors cannot make arguments "calculated to inflame the passions or prejudices of the jury (ABA, 1993);" however, not all emotional appeals are impermissible. For example, emotional victim impact statements are allowed during the sentencing phase to urge tougher penalties (*Payne v. Tennessee*, 1991), and gruesome details of the victim's death are typically allowed as evidence of the gravity of the crime (*Tucker v. Zant*, 1984).

Generally, arguments are restricted only when they prejudice the jury against the defendant (*Gregg v. Georgia*, 1976; see Brooks, 1999 for review). Further, remarks prejudicially affect the rights of the defendant when they have "so infected the trial with unfairness as to make the resulting conviction a denial of due process (*Donnelly v. DeChristoforo*, 1974. p. 1871)." Further, "a prosecutor may not make an appeal to the jury that is directed to passion or prejudice rather than to reason and to an understanding of the law (*Cunningham v. Zant*, 1991, p. 1020; *U.S. v. Rodriguez*, 1985, p. 1560)." Some courts have determined that religious arguments cross this line (*Cunningham v. Zant*, 1991; *Ice v. Commonwealth*, 1984; *U.S. v. Giry*, 1987; *People v. Rohn*, 1980).

One court has characterized the use of religious appeals as "a deliberate attempt to destroy the objectivity and impartiality of the finder of fact so as to cause the verdict to be a product of emotion rather than reflective judgment (*Commonwealth v. Chambers*, 1991, p. 643)." Other courts have determined that religious appeals are highly prejudicial (*Jones v. Kemp*, 1989; *Sandoval v. Calderon*, 2000; *State v. Wangberg*, 1965) and are unnecessary or irrelevant appeals to jurors' religious beliefs (*Carruthers v. State*, 2000; *Gibson v. State*, 1972; *U.S. v. Giry*, 1987). In general, these courts have determined that religious appeals jeopardize the defendant's right to a fair trial because they lead jurors to rely on their emotions instead of the law.

Legality of Defense Appeals

Courts that have prohibited religious appeals by the defense attorneys have reasoned that such arguments are improper because they prevent jurors from considering the evidence or because they contradict legislative statutes regarding the death penalty (*Commonwealth v. Daniels*, 1994; *Ice v. Commonwealth*, 1984).

The court in *Commonwealth v. Daniels* (1994) found religious appeals impermissible because they disrupt the jurors' duty to consider the evidence and determine the sentence. Appeals also go beyond evidence of the defendant's character. The *Daniels* defense attorney argued that God teaches us mercy, gave the example of Cain and

Abel, and professed, "if we cannot create life, what legal authority do we have to extinguish it?" The court determined that a religious appeal is "improper when it goes beyond the bounds of consideration of the character and the record of the accused" (1994, p. 1183). Similarly, another court recognized that the defense should be allowed some latitude in presenting mitigation, but this latitude does not extend to use of religion as a factor weighing against the death sentence (*Sandoval v. Calderon*, 2000).

Two courts have determined that religious appeals forbidding the death penalty are impermissible because such an argument would be counter to the law in the state, which provides that the death penalty is an appropriate punishment in some cases (*Commonwealth v. Daniels*, 1994; *Ice v. Commonwealth*, 1984). The court in *Ice* stated, "The law specifies when the death penalty is appropriate, and neither the prosecutor nor the defense counsel should be permitted to adduce evidence as to how this case should be decided on religious grounds. Evidence…about religious convictions as to the death penalty violates the rule excluding evidence where its probative value is slight and far outweighed by its inflammatory nature (1984, p. 676)." In sum, these courts have determined that religious appeals are improper because they distract jurors and encourage verdicts based on emotions and extra-legal factors.

## CONCLUSION

A review of the court cases which have made rulings regarding appeals indicates a wide variety of rules. Conflicting rules are not merely a matter of separate jurisdictions being faced with different religious appeals. This is evident in the fact that different courts have reached opposing decisions regarding identical or similar arguments. For example, some courts have declared the "eye for an eye" argument proper (*Green v. State*, 1996; *State v. Shurn*, 2003; *Thompson v. State*, 1991), whereas others have deemed it impermissible (*Hammond v. State*, 1995; *People v. Wash*, 1993). Similarly, the "millstones for child murderers" appeal has been approved by some courts

(*State v. Holden*, 1997; *State v. Sidden*, 1997), but found impermissible by others (*Commonwealth v. Brown*, 1998; *Long v. State*, 1994). These discrepancies are the products of divergent rules that courts have adopted regarding religious appeals. Until the Supreme Court makes the definitive judgment regarding the permissibility of appeals, lower courts are likely to remain sharply divided.

# CHAPTER 7

# Research Questions Surrounding Religious Appeals

From the various Biblical interpretations offered by prosecutors and defense attorneys, it seems like the Bible both requires and forbids capital punishment, depending on which side of the adversarial system the attorney is representing. So what is a juror to make out of these differing interpretations? Do jurors let religious appeals influence their decision-making in legally impermissible ways? Many such questions can be answered through experimental research, which is the goal of the studies reported in the following chapters. These questions concern whether appeals affect jurors' ability to weigh aggravators and mitigators, whether appeals affect perceived responsibility for the sentencing decision and whether both prosecution and defense appeals affect jurors. Additional questions raised in the current research include whether Cognitive-Experiential Self-Theory (CEST), a dual processing model, can explain how jurors make decisions and whether individual differences influence decision-making and the effectiveness of appeals. In order to answer some of these questions, two studies were conducted and will be reported in Chapters 9 and 10. This chapter summarizes the general research questions surrounding religious appeals.

The research described in Chapters 9 and 10 will address six general questions: 1) Do appeals affect jurors' ability to weigh aggravators and mitigators? 2) Does Cognitive-Experiential Self-Theory (CEST) explain differences in decision-making? 3) Do appeals reduce perceived responsibility for the sentencing decision? 4) Do both prosecutorial and defense appeals affect decision-making? 5) Do different types of CEST information processing directives affect jury decision-making? 6) Do individual differences (e.g., a juror's religious affiliation or gender) affect decision-making?

## DO APPEALS AFFECT JURORS' ABILITY TO WEIGH AGGRAVATORS AND MITIGATORS?

Some courts that have found religious appeals impermissible have suggested that such arguments lead jurors to make decisions based on emotion and prevent jurors from properly considering aggravating and mitigating factors (*Carruthers v. State*, 2000; *Cunningham v. Zant*, 1991; *Sandoval v. Calderon*, 2000). This research will investigate whether dual processing systems provide an explanation of the mechanisms by which religious appeals may influence jurors' decisions.

## DOES COGNITIVE-EXPERIENTIAL SELF-THEORY (CEST) EXPLAIN DIFFERENCES IN DECISION-MAKING?

Cognitive-Experiential Self-Theory (CEST) is a dual processing model that posits that individuals process information through two distinct systems (Epstein, 1990; 1994; Epstein, et al., 1992). The "rational" system is analytic, effortful and logical, while the "experiential" system is automatic, effortless and based on affect. According to CEST, an individual who experiences an emotionally significant event is likely to respond experientially instead of rationally, making it difficult to make logical judgments. For example, individuals processing rationally will outperform individuals processing experientially on tasks such as the "Linda problem (Tversky & Kanheman, 1983)." In the Linda problem, individuals processing experientially are more likely than those processing rationally to make conjunction errors (i.e., stating that the probability of two events occurring together is greater than one of the events occurring alone). This problem and the other two CEST measures (Epstein, 1992) that will be used in the studies reported in Chapters 9 and 10 are attached as Appendix A, and are described in greater detail in the Scoring portion of the Results section of Chapter 9.

As applied to religious appeals, CEST would suggest that, due to their emotional nature, religious appeals will lead to experiential processing. CEST suggests that jurors in capital cases who process information experientially will perform less rationally in the sense that they will be less able to properly weigh aggravating and mitigating factors. Participants processing experientially will use emotions as a guide for making their sentencing decision instead of closely following the jury instructions that explain how to weigh aggravator and mitigators. In comparison, participants who do not receive an appeal will be able to process more rationally and will be better able to weigh aggravators and mitigators as instructed.

The CEST model can determine whether the courts are correct in their assumption that emotional religious appeals make it difficult for jurors to make sentencing decisions in a legally required manner (i.e., by weighing aggravating and mitigating circumstances). CEST would suggest that religious appeals activate the experiential system, leading jurors to act on their emotions rather than logic. Absent appeals, jurors will be better able to make logical decisions because they can better access the rational processing system.

## DO APPEALS REDUCE PERCEIVED RESPONSIBILITY FOR THE SENTENCING DECISION?

The second research question investigates whether appeals diminish jurors' sense of responsibility for the sentencing decision. As some courts have noted, religious appeals may lead jurors to feel less responsible for the decision if they believe the decision is required by the Bible or God (*Carruthers v. State*, 2000; *People v. Wash*, 1993; *Sandoval v. Calderon*, 2000). If this is so, then such appeals violate the Caldwell rule, which states that it is "constitutionally impermissible to rest a death sentence on a determination made by a sentencer who has been led to believe that the responsibility for determining the appropriateness for the defendant's death rests elsewhere (*Caldwell v. Mississippi*, 1985, p. 328)." Thus, it is important to determine whether religious appeals undermine the juror's sense of responsibility for making the death penalty decision.

CEST also provides insight into how responsibility may be affected by religious appeals. Once participants have been exposed to emotional arguments, the experiential system kicks in, reducing rational decision-making. Using emotions as a guide, participants will be less able to comprehend and follow instructions, and thus will not fully understand that the responsibility is theirs alone. Additionally, heightened emotion will cause jurors to avoid responsibility because they do not want to think about personally causing someone's death. When asked which entities are responsible for the sentencing decision, jurors experiencing religious appeals will use the appeal as a mental "shortcut" because their highly emotional state leaves them unwilling or unable to accept responsibility.

In sum, religious appeals give jurors an easy target to blame for the sentencing decision. Jurors can avoid the negative feelings associated with sentencing by placing the blame on God or on Biblical law instead of accepting the blame themselves. Thus, it is possible that experiencing emotional arguments (and hence processing experientially) may lead jurors to feel less responsibility for the sentencing decision.

## DO BOTH PROSECUTORIAL AND DEFENSE APPEALS AFFECT DECISION-MAKING?

Another area of interest concerns the comparison between appeals used by the prosecution and the defense. As some courts have determined that the prosecution can use religious appeals if the defense does first (*Boyd v. French*, 1998; *Commonwealth v. Cook*, 1996), it is important to determine the effects of both appeals used by the defense and appeals used by the prosecution. It is possible that appeals used by the prosecution may not influence processing and decision-making in the same manner as appeals by the defense.

Prosecutors who use religious appeals assume that appeals for retribution will sway jurors to sentence the defendant to death, and defense attorneys assume that their religious appeals encourage jurors to give the defendant a lesser sentence. Some research indicates that these might not be safe assumptions, however. Johnson (1985) found that jurors were more punitive toward a defendant who used religious evidence than a defendant who did not, suggesting that a defense appeal may have the opposite effect as intended. Defendants who used religion as a defense were perceived as more responsible for their crimes, were more likely to be found guilty and received longer sentences compared to defendants who did not offer religious evidence. Johnson suggested that jurors might expect Christian individuals to act with a certain level of moral responsibility. Because hurting others violates this expectancy, jurors become incensed by a defendant who tries to use religion as a reason to get a lighter sentence. These negative emotions lead jurors to treat the defendant more punitively.

Although the defendant in the current study will not be using evidence of his religiosity as a defense as in the

Johnson (1985) study, jurors may still perceive the defendant as mis-using religion in order to get a lighter sentence. The emotions aroused by mercy appeals may lead to experiential processing and affect juror decision-making, just like their retributive counterparts. However, instead of using the mercy appeal to guide their decision, participants may use their negative impression of the defendant (based on his misappropriation of religion in his appeal) to guide their judgments, resulting in an increased number of death sentences.

## DO DIFFERENT TYPES OF CEST INFORMATION PROCESSING DIRECTIVES AFFECT JURY DECISION-MAKING?

It is also of interest to determine whether directives on how to make the sentencing decision can affect the type of processing the juror uses to make a verdict. CEST predicts that instructions to process either experientially or rationally could affect the way jurors process trial information. During closing arguments, an attorney could give jurors an experiential directive (e.g., "Make the sentencing decision using your gut feelings") or a rational directive (e.g., "Make the sentencing decision by closely following the instructions"). Such directives could be important trial tactics. For instance, an attorney may give an appeal along with a directive to process experientially to promote jurors' reliance on the appeal. Conversely, after an attorney has made an emotional appeal, the opposing attorney may employ a rational directive in an attempt to counter the appeal.

## DO INDIVIDUAL DIFFERENCES AFFECT JURY DECISION-MAKING?

The final research question addresses the issue of individual differences among jurors: Do individual characteristics of jurors (e.g., having a strong religious background or holding certain religious convictions) affect decisions or make jurors more likely to be influenced by religious appeals?  As briefly discussed in Chapter 3, some religious variables are related to attitudes towards punishment.

It is reasonable to assume that there are certain characteristics that may affect the degree to which religious appeals influence jurors. As individuals are socialized by religious affiliation, they may use their religious beliefs as cues in the decision-making process.  In a case study of a jury in a criminal trial, Howard & Redfering (1983) found that many intercorrelated religious belief variables were significantly related to a guilty vote, such as being particularly interested in religion, believing in a Divine plan and purpose, and believing in life after death.  This study found that religiously conservative jurors were more likely to vote for conviction.  Thus, religious beliefs were important factors in jury deliberation and decision-making (Howard & Redfering, 1983).

Other research indicates that the relationship between religion and support for the death penalty is a complex, dynamic relationship that may be affected by factors such as the type of religion one practices, the amount of time one spends on religious activities, or whether one believes the Bible should be interpreted literally (Young, 1992).

Although there is little research investigating religious attitudes of actual jurors, there is research that has investigated related attitudes of the public, mock jurors, and judges.  Such research, while not exactly on target, does provide some information about how real jurors' religiosity might affect their verdicts.

Religious Ideology

An individual's understanding of his religion's teachings concerning the death penalty may affect his decisions.  For example, jurors who believe that their religion supports the death penalty may be more influenced by a prosecutor's use of the "eye for an eye" appeal than a juror who does not believe his religion supports the death penalty.  The similarity between the defendant's and jurors' religiosity may also affect jurors' decisions. Kerr and colleagues (1995) found that both Jewish and Christian mock jurors were more lenient to defendants who were members of their own religious group than to defendants of another religious group. Additionally, Jewish mock jurors are more lenient overall than Christians (Kerr, et al., 1995), while Catholics are less supportive of the death penalty than other religions (Miller & Hawyard, under review; O'Neil, Patry & Penrod, 2004). Other studies, however, have found that religious denomination has no significant influence on death penalty attitudes or sentencing verdicts (Gonzalez-Perez, 2001; Miller and Bornstein, under review).

Fundamentalism

A study by Young (1992) indicated that individuals who were members of fundamentalist churches were more punitive than members of other churches. The author suggested that this was because fundamentalists are more likely to hold others responsible for their actions. Similarly, Grasmick and colleagues (Grasmick, Cochran, Bursik & Kimpel, 1993; Grasmick, Davenport, Chamlin & Bursik, 1992) have determined that there is a positive relationship between Christian fundamentalism, support for the death penalty, and attitudes toward punishment. Other studies (Miller & Bornstein, under review; Leiber and Woodrick, 1997), failed to replicate this relationship between fundamentalism and punitiveness. Miller and Hayward (under review) also found that supporters and opponents of the death penalty did not differ on a fundamentalism scale, suggesting that the relationship needs to be investigated further.

Evangelism

Young (1992) compared individuals on the basis of evangelism, defined by their "yes" or "no" answer to the question, "Have you ever tried to encourage someone to believe in Jesus Christ or to accept Jesus Christ as his or her savior?" Evangelicals (i.e., those who were answered "yes") were less likely to support the death penalty. Evangelicals were said to be motivated to bring others to find salvation in Jesus Christ. Accordingly, they may be opposed to the death penalty because it represents a lost opportunity to lead the defendant to Jesus. Other researchers have found that evangelicals are actually more punitive (Miller & Bornstein, under review; Songer and Tabrizi, 1999). Songer and Tabrizi (2000) compared voting behavior of evangelical and non-evangelical judges. The researchers discovered that evangelicals were significantly more likely to vote to uphold the death penalty than mainline Protestants or Jewish judges and were marginally more supportive of the death penalty than Catholic judges. Thus, this relationship also needs to be investigated further.

Devotionalism

Similarly, an individual's level of devotionalism may affect sentencing decisions. Young (1992) found that devotionalism, defined as how often the participant attends religious services, prays, and reads the Bible, was related to reduced support for the death penalty. While some studies indicate that individuals who are high in devotionalism are less punitive (Bjarnason & Welch, 2004; Young, 1992), another found that mock jurors who were highly devotional were more punitive (Johnson, 1985).

Gonzalez-Perez (2001) found that religiosity was strongly associated with support for the death penalty; specifically, those who most strongly support the death penalty indicated that they attended church at least once weekly. Two other studies (Miller and Bornstein, under review; Miller and Hayward, under review) found no relationship between devotionalism and punitiveness. Miller and Hayward (under review) found that death penalty opponents scored higher than supporters on a devotionalism scale, but the groups did not differ on the frequency of engaging in religious activities. Greer and colleagues (2005) found a complex relationship between devotionalism and feelings of vengeance. Intrinsic religious orientation was negatively related to self-reports of vengeance and extrinsic religious orientation was positively correlated to these self-reports. Specifically, the authors found that those who consistently donated to their church were more retaliatory, yet those who participated in a number of church activities and had higher church attendance were found to be less retaliatory.

Literal Interpretism

Additionally, individuals who interpret the Bible literally may be more influenced by Biblical appeals than those without that belief. "Literal interpreters" are individuals who believe that "the Bible is the actual word of God and is to be taken literally, word for word (Young, 1992, p. 82)." Several studies have found a positive relationship between belief in a strict interpretation of the Bible and support for the death penalty (Leiber & Woodrick, 1997; Miller & Bornstein, under review; Miller & Hayward, under review, Young, 1992). Such studies indicate that literal interpreters may be more likely to sentence a defendant to death and to rely on religious appeals. In an investigation of attitudes towards punishments, Applegate et. al (2000) found that literal interpreters were less likely to believe that rehabilitation was an important goal of prisons and generally were less supportive of treatments for prisoners.

Rational-Experiential Inventory (REI)

In addition to these religious individual characteristics, there may be differences in decision-making based on how a person generally processes information. Epstein and colleagues (Epstein, et al., 1996) developed a scale called the Rational-Experiential Inventory (REI) that measures individual differences in modes of processing as defined by CEST. Individuals who tend to process information experientially are more prone to making errors in logic problems (e.g., the "Linda" problem described above) than individuals who tend to process rationally. In the current study, experiential thinkers are expected to be affected by appeals to emotions, such as religious appeals, more than rational thinkers.

Gender and Age

Gender and age could also influence decision-making in capital punishment sentencing trials. Previous studies have found that men were more in favor of capital punishment than women (Sandys & McGarrell, 1995; Whitehead & Blankenship, 2000), although other studies found no such relationship (Lester, Maggioncalda-Aretz & Stark 1997; Valliant & Oliver, 1997). The relationship between support for capital punishment and age has not been widely explored, though there is some evidence that younger individuals are more supportive of capital punishment than older individuals (Lester, et al., 1997).

CONCLUSION

As discussed above, religious variables can affect jurors' attitudes towards punishment and verdicts. In addition to the effect on verdicts, it is also possible that religion has other effects on jurors. For example, religious jurors may base their decisions on Biblical teachings rather than solely on state law and judge's instructions. On the other hand, less religious jurors may be more able to ignore these extra-legal religious influences. Such reliance on Biblical authority poses a threat to proper juror decision-making, as it is may encourage less reliance on legal factors and more reliance on extra-legal factors. Thus, religious factors could affect several aspects of juror's decisions.

The studies presented in Chapters 9 and 10 are designed to answer a host of questions surrounding religion in death penalty sentencing trials. Through the use of two experimental studies, it can be determined whether Biblical appeals used by attorneys in closing arguments affect jurors' sentencing decisions or their ability to properly weigh aggravators and mitigators. The studies can also determine if the psychological processes involved in jurors' decisions can be explained by Cognitive-Experiential Self Theory (CEST). Further, the studies will determine whether religious appeals affect jurors' sense of personal responsibility for the sentencing decisions and investigate the relationships between individual differences and sentencing decisions (i.e., life in prison or death penalty). Such information will be useful to judges, attorneys and policy-makers who make decisions about the use of Biblical appeals.

# CHAPTER 8

# Overview of Experimental Studies

The studies described in the next two chapters are designed to investigate whether religious appeals, as well as equivalent non-religious appeals, increase experiential processing, decrease sensitivity to aggravators and mitigators, and reduce perceived responsibility for the sentencing decision. Additionally, this research will determine whether processing type can be influenced by directives on how to process information (either rationally or experientially) while making the sentencing decision. Finally, this study will investigate a number of individual differences, such as an individual's religious orientation and level of devotionalism, which may affect verdicts and interact with religious appeals.

Specifically, this research will address the following questions: 1) Do religious appeals lead jurors to process experientially instead of rationally? 2) Do religious appeals affect jurors' ability to weigh aggravators and mitigators? 3) Do religious appeals give jurors a diminished sense of responsibility for the sentencing decision? 4) Do directives instructing jurors to process rationally or experientially affect juror decision-making? 5) Do non-religious appeals have the same effects as equivalent religious appeals? 6) Are certain types of jurors (e.g., those with strong religious backgrounds or those who adhere to particular religions) more likely to be influenced by religious appeals? 7) Do both prosecutorial and defense appeals affect juror decision-making?

The following chapters will report results of two studies: Study One, reported in Chapter 9, investigated the effects of prosecutorial appeals, while Study Two, reported in Chapter 10, investigated the effects of defense appeals. Both studies examined the effects of rational and experiential directives. Through experimental manipulation, these two studies will inform courts about the effects of religious appeals.

# Study One: The Use of Religious Appeals by Prosecutors

Study One investigated the effects of retributive appeals used by prosecutors. This study was designed to determine whether religious retributive appeals, as well as non-religious retributive appeals, lead to experiential processing, a reduction in sensitivity to aggravators and mitigators, and a diminished sense of responsibility for the sentencing decision. Additionally, this study was intended to determine if directives instructing jurors to process rationally or experientially affect processing style and decision-making. Finally, this study investigated whether individual differences such as evangelism and fundamentalism affect jurors' decision-making.

In Study One, participants read a trial summary and acted as mock jurors deciding a sentence in a death penalty case. The trial summary contained either a religious retributive appeal, a non-religious retributive appeal or no appeal. The trial summary case facts were varied to contain either high mitigators (i.e., the case facts favor a life sentence) or high aggravators (i.e., the case facts favor a death sentence). Finally, the trial summary contained a directive from the attorney to process the information rationally, a directive to process experientially, or no directive. Thus, the design was a 3 (appeal) X 2 (case type) X 3 (directive) between subjects design.

## HYPOTHESES FOR STUDY ONE

This section will present hypotheses for the independent variables (i.e., appeals, processing directives and case type), including predictions for interactions among these variables, followed by the predictions for individual differences.

### Independent Variable One: Appeals

#### CEST Dependent Measures

Participants who receive religious appeals are expected to process more experientially, whereas participants who do not receive appeals are expected to process more rationally. The mode of processing will be measured by traditional CEST measures such as the "Linda" problem. Non-religious appeals are expected to have similar, yet weaker, effects as religious appeals.

#### Verdicts

It is expected that individuals receiving appeals (either religious or non-religious) will issue more death sentences overall than those not receiving appeals.

#### Perceived Responsibility

It is expected that jurors receiving appeals (both religious and non-religious) will feel less personal responsibility for the sentencing decision than participants who do not receive appeals. Compared to the no-appeal group, participants in the religious appeal group will be more likely to place the responsibility for the sentencing decision on the Bible or God.

## General Feelings of Retribution and Mercy

Based on Johnson's (1985) findings, it is expected that jurors receiving a religious appeal will be more supportive of general notions of retribution or "pay back" for crime, and less supportive of forgiveness than participants receiving a non-religious appeal, and that both groups receiving appeals will be more supportive of retribution and less supportive of forgiveness than the no-appeal group.

## Independent Variable Two: Processing Directives

## CEST Dependent Measures

Rational directives (e.g., "Make the sentencing decision by closely following the jury instructions") will increase rational processing and reduce experiential processing as measured by the CEST task. Conversely, receiving a directive to process experientially (e.g., "Make the sentencing decisions using your gut feelings") will reduce rational processing and increase experiential processing as measured by the CEST tasks.

## Verdicts

Although the processing directives tell participants how to make the decision, they do not tell the participant which decision (i.e., life or death) to make. Thus, no predictions are made for the main effect of processing directives on verdicts. However, the directive variable is predicted to interact with religious appeals, as described below.

## Perception of Personal Responsibility

It is expected that receiving a rational directive will increase perceived personal responsibility, while receiving an experiential directive will decrease the amount of perceived responsibility. The rational directive emphasizes the importance of following the judge's instructions, which note that the responsibility for sentencing lies with the jurors. On the other hand, the experiential directive encourages jurors to follow their emotions, which may lead them to blame others (e.g., the judge or the defendant) for the decision.

Independent Variable Three: Case Type

This manipulation is not expected to affect any of the dependent measures except verdict.

<u>Verdict</u>

Because the jury instructions emphasize the importance of weighing aggravators and mitigators in determining a sentence, it is expected that individuals reading the trial summary with high aggravators will be more likely to vote for the death penalty than individuals reading the trial summary with high mitigators.

Interactions between Independent Variables

<u>Interaction between Appeals and Case Type</u>

It is expected that jurors receiving religious appeals (and thus processing more experientially) will not be as sensitive to aggravators and mitigators as will jurors not receiving religious appeals (and thus processing more rationally). Thus, an interaction is expected between case type (i.e., high aggravators or high mitigators) and the type of appeal (i.e., religious, non-religious or none). Participants receiving retributive religious appeals will be more likely to vote for death regardless of whether they received a trial summary that favored the death penalty or a summary that favored a life sentence.

     On the other hand, participants not receiving religious appeals will be more sensitive to the aggravators and mitigators present in the trial summary: In the no-appeal condition, participants who receive the trial summary favoring a death sentence (i.e., high aggravators) will be more likely to sentence the defendant to death than participants receiving the trial summary favoring a life sentence (i.e., high mitigators). Participants receiving non-religious appeals will behave similarly to those in the religious appeal condition and will therefore be less sensitive to aggravators and mitigators than participants who do not receive appeals, although this effect is expected to be weaker than the same effect for religious appeals.

<u>Interaction between Processing Directives and Case Type</u>

Experiential processing directives are expected to induce experiential processing in the same manner as religious appeals. Thus, the predictions for this interaction parallel those for the interaction between appeals and case type stated above: Participants receiving experiential directives will be less sensitive to aggravators and mitigators than participants receiving either no directive or a rational directive, and the rational directive group will be the most sensitive to aggravators and mitigators.

<u>Interaction between Processing Directives and Appeals</u>

Because a main effect of processing directive on verdicts is not predicted, the prediction for this interaction is speculative. However, it is expected that, for individuals receiving an appeal (either religious or non-religious), those also receiving an experiential directive will issue more death sentences than participants in either the control (no directive) or rational directive condition, who will issue the fewest death sentences. Participants in the no-appeal (control) condition will not be affected by directives. Thus, there is a predicted effect of directive in the religious and non-religious appeal conditions, but not the control condition.

## Three-way-interaction of Appeal, Processing Directive and Case Type

Although the three-way interaction will be included in the model, no prediction is made for this interaction.

## Individual Differences as Independent Variables

### Religious Attitude Measures

Based on previous research demonstrating a relationship between religious beliefs and attitudes toward punishment (e.g., Young, 1992), it is predicted that individuals high in fundamentalism, low in devotionalism, low on evangelism, and those who believe in a strict translation of the Bible will be more likely to award the death penalty than participants without these characteristics.

### Rational-Experiential Inventory

The REI contains two scales, the Faith in Intuition scale (FI), which measures the individual's tendency to process information experientially, and the Need for Cognition scale (NFC), which measures the tendency to process rationally. It is expected that individuals who process more experientially on the FI scale will perform worse on the CEST measure and will be less sensitive to aggravators and mitigators than those who process less experientially. On the other hand, individuals who process more rationally on the NFC scale will perform better on the CEST scale and be more sensitive to aggravators and mitigators than individuals who process less rationally.

## METHOD

### Participants

Participants were 204 undergraduate students recruited from the University of Nebraska-Lincoln who received extra credit in their psychology course for their participation and 99 community participants who received $10 for their participation. Community participants were recruited through posters hung in public areas, through email listserves of local volunteer organizations, and through booths at community events.

The final sample consisted of 303 participants (92 males and 211 females) with a mean age of 28.0 years (SD = 12.9 years). The demographic characteristics of the participants are contained in Table 1. The community and student participants did not differ in gender ($X^2$ (2) = 3.54, p > .05), race ($X^2$ (5) = 10.58, p > .05), religious background ($X^2$ (7) = 13.92, p > .05), or verdict ($X^2$ (1) = 1.47, p > .05). Further, there was no difference in the number of participants who were eliminated for death qualification ($X^2$ (1) = 3.44, p > .05; see Materials, below).

The groups were also similar in scores on the devotionalism scale (t (293) = .163, p > .05), fundamentalism scale (t (293) = .435, p > .05), and evangelism scale (t (290) = 1.50, p > .05). Not surprisingly, the community group was significantly older (M = 41.9 years) than the student group (M = 21.4 years, t (298) = 19.42, p < .05).

Since students and non-students did not differ in significant ways (other than age), the groups were combined for further analyses.

## Design

The design was a 2 (case facts: High aggravators/high mitigators) X 3 (retributive appeal: Religious/non-religious/control) X 3 (processing directive: Experiential/rational/ control) design. Each cell had an average of 16.8 participants, with cell sizes ranging from 14 to 20 participants.

## Table 1. Comparison of Students and Non-Students

| | | Students (N=204) | Non-Students (N=99) | Overall (N=303) | Final Sample (N=257) |
|---|---|---|---|---|---|
| Verdict | Life | 69% | 62% | 66% | 63% |
| Gender | Male | 34% | 23% | 30% | 31% |
| Age* | Mean | 21.35 | 41.93 | 28 | 28.3 |
| | Median | 20 | 40 | 22 | 22 |
| | SD | 4.5 | 13.7 | 12.9 | 13.1 |
| Racial/ ethnic background | White | 85% | 95% | 88% | 89% |
| | Black | 3% | - | 2% | 2% |
| | Asian | 4% | - | 3% | 2% |
| | Hispanic | 1% | 1% | 1% | 2% |
| | Native American | 1% | 2% | 2% | 2% |
| | Other | 4% | 1% | 3% | 4% |
| Religious Affiliation | Catholic | 25% | 15% | 22% | 21% |
| | Protestant | 47% | 50% | 48% | 50% |
| | Other | 6% | 6% | 6% | 6% |
| | No specific faith | 12% | 24% | 16% | 17% |
| | Atheist/ Agnostic | 6% | 4% | 6% | 5% |
| Religious Scale Means | Fundamentalism | 30.47 | 30 | 30.32 | 30.63 |
| | Evangelism | 22.95 | 21.56 | 22.51 | 22.41 |
| | Devotionalism | 28.35 | 28.52 | 28.41 | 28.08 |
| Death Qualification | Eliminated | 17% | 9.20% | 15% | N/A |

*p < .05 for comparison between students and non-students

Materials

## Death Qualification Questionnaire

Before reading the trial summary, participants were death qualified based on the standard established in *Wainwright v. Witt* (1985). They were asked to indicate whether their sentiments about the death penalty were so strong that they would seriously affect them as a juror and prevent or substantially impair their performance (see Appendix E). According to this legal standard, a juror who answers this item in the affirmative may be excluded from jury service.

## Trial Summary

The written trial summary described the penalty phase of a capital trial. The summary was approximately 1800 words long and contained a summary of the case facts and closing arguments. The summary was based loosely on *State v. Daniels* (1994), a North Carolina case in which a man was sentenced to death for murdering his aunt. During the sentencing phase of the actual trial, both the prosecutor and defense attorney used religious appeals. The defendant appealed, claiming that the prosecutor's use of religious appeals was prejudicial. The Supreme Court of North Carolina affirmed the death sentence and held that Biblical arguments are within the permissible scope of closing arguments. The Court also considered that the defendant had used religious appeals in his argument in making the final decision that the prosecutor's religious appeals were proper. The U.S. Supreme Court denied the defendant's petition for writ of certiorari (*Daniels v. North Carolina*, 1995), and the U.S. Court of Appeals upheld a subsequent denial of a petition for writ of habeas corpus (*Daniels v. Lee*, 2003). The defendant was executed November 14, 2003.

The nature of the crime was manipulated through the inclusion or exclusion of aggravators (e.g., the crime was committed for pecuniary gain) and mitigators (e.g., the defendant confessed to the crime and cooperated with authorities). The trial summary contained one of two fact patterns (see Appendix A). One trial summary favored the death penalty (four aggravators and two mitigators), and the other summary favored a sentence of life in prison without the possibility of parole (two aggravators and four mitigators). This manipulation created a "rational" answer to the sentencing question and determined if jurors receiving appeals (and/or processing experientially) were less sensitive to the aggravators and mitigators than jurors not receiving appeals (and /or processing rationally).

The trial summary also included closing arguments (see Appendix B). The prosecution's argument contained a religious appeal (e.g., "The Bible says men should be punished "an eye for an eye"), a non-religious appeal (e.g., "The law is intended to make sure that criminals are punished appropriately for their crimes"), or no appeal (control condition). This manipulation determined whether a religious appeal was more influential to jurors' decision-making than an equivalent, non-religious appeal.

Finally, the closing argument also contained either an experiential directive (e.g., "Make the sentencing decision using your gut feelings"), a rational directive (e.g., "Make the sentencing decision by closely following the instructions"), or no directive (control condition). This manipulation determined whether such directives influenced processing type, and whether such directives interacted with the religious appeals.

### Instructions and Verdict Form

The instructions and verdict form were based on those used in North Carolina (See Appendix C and Appendix D).

## Dependent Measures Survey

The dependent measures survey (see Appendix E) contained measures of:
- The participant's sentencing decision (life in prison without parole or a death sentence)
- One question measuring how certain the participant is of his/her verdict (7 point scale)
- One question asking participants the degree to which they agree that the defendant is guilty (7 point scale)
- One question concerning the degree to which participants' attitudes toward the death penalty were based on their religious beliefs (7 point scale)
- One manipulation check for instruction comprehension concerning whether the participant believed that state law requires the death penalty in some cases (yes/no)
- Eight questions concerning the amount of influence eight elements (judge's instructions/state law, Biblical authority, defense attorney arguments, prosecution arguments, evidence presented in the case, your personal religious beliefs, your personal feelings about the death penalty, other) had on the sentencing decision (7 point scale)
- Seven questions concerning the amount of responsibility (7 point scale) for the decision the participant assigned to seven entities (judge's instructions, state law, Biblical authority, juror (you), defendant, chance, the victim, other)
- An open-ended question asking if there are other factors that influenced the sentencing decision
- Two questions concerning whether criminals deserve mercy and forgiveness (7 point scale)
- ) Two questions concerning whether criminals deserve the death penalty and "pay back" for their crimes (7 point scale)
- One question regarding whether it is acceptable to invoke religion in a criminal trial (7 point scale)

• Two questions concerning whether they believed God requires or supports the death penalty (7 point scale)

• One question, for participants who feel that God requires the death penalty for murderers, asking whether this requirement applies to all murders equally (yes/no)

• Two questions concerning whether they have previously served as jurors in an actual civil or criminal trial (yes/no), and if so, how many times (open ended)

• A blank for participants to write their age

• A question about gender (check Male or Female)

• Two questions about student status (yes/no) and if yes, a blank to write major course of study

• One question about racial/ethnic background (check African-American, Asian American, Hispanic American, Native American, White American or Other)

• One question about religious background (check Catholic, Protestant, Jewish, Hindu, Buddhist, Muslim, Other, Atheist, Agnostic or "I believe in God but do not have a particular faith")

• One question regarding how closely the participant follows his/her religion (7 point scale with "n/a" option)

• One question concerning whether the participant's religion forbids or supports the death penalty (7 point scale with "n/a" and "don't know" options)

• One question regarding how often s/he engages in religious activity (with 6 options from "More than once a day" to "Never")

• A six-item devotionalism measure (7 point scale; Putney & Middleton, 1961)

• A six-item fundamentalism measure (7 point scale; Putney & Middleton, 1961)

• A six-item evangelism measure (7 point scale; Putney & Middleton, 1961)

• A one-item evangelism scale asking if the participant has ever encouraged someone to believe in Jesus Christ (yes/no; Young, 1992)

• A one-item literal interpretism measure asking if the participant believes that the Bible is the actual word of God and is to be taken literally (yes/no; Young, 1992)

- The 10-item Rational-Experiential Inventory (REI; 5 point scale; Epstein, et al., 1996)

The CEST measures consisted of three questions:

- The "Linda" problem (Tversky & Kaheman, 1983) mentioned in the Introduction and described in more detail below (see "Scoring")
- Two other CEST measures (9 point scale, described in more detail below; Epstein, 1992)

Procedure

Participants completed the survey either in person, or received the survey through email. In-person participants were given a paper copy of the survey by the researcher. Email participants were emailed a survey that was identical to the surveys given to the in-person participants. The email participants then completed the survey and emailed or printed and mailed the survey back to the researchers.

<u>Email versus in person surveys</u>

Some participants completed the survey in person ($N = 232$), while others were sent an email containing a copy of the survey, which they completed and returned ($N = 71$). The email and in-person groups did not differ in gender ($X^2 (1) = .017$, $p > .05$), race ($X^2 (5) = 5.78$, $p > .05$), religious background ($X^2 (7) = 6.0$, $p > .05$), or verdict ($X^2 (1) = .298$, $p > .05$). Further, there was no difference in the number of participants who were eliminated for death qualification ($X^2 (1) = .281$, $p > .05$). The groups did not differ in scores on the devotionalism scale ($t (293) = .399$, $p > .05$) or the evangelism scale ($t (290) = .911$, $p > .05$), nor did they differ in age ($t (298) = 1.85$, $p > .05$). They did differ, however, on the fundamentalism scale ($t (293) = 2.46$, $p < .05$). The in-person group ($M = 31.04$) scored significantly higher than the email group ($M = 28.06$) on the fundamentalism scale. Since email and in-person did not differ in significant ways (other than the fundamentalism scale), the groups were combined for further analyses.

Participants were told (by the researcher or in the email instructions) that they would be completing two unrelated studies: A study in which they would be asked to be a juror in a death penalty trial and a separate study in which they would complete three short judgment tasks. After reading and signing consent forms, participants read one version of the trial summary and jury instructions. Jurors were told that the defendant had already been found guilty and their task was to sentence the defendant. They then completed the dependent measures questionnaire. After participants completed the jury task, they were told that there was another brief, unrelated study for them to complete. They then completed the CEST measures. When they were finished with the CEST measures, they were provided with written and oral debriefing and thanked for their participation.

RESULTS

Death Qualification

In order to make the results more externally generalizable, participants were death-qualified using the Witt death qualification question. Fifteen percent of the sample (n= 44) indicated that their attitudes toward the death penalty were so strong that they would seriously affect their performance as a juror. Two other participants did not answer the death qualification question. These 46 participants were eliminated from the remainder of the analyses.

The final sample consisted of 257 participants (31% male) with ages ranging from 18-75 (mean age 28.3, SD= 13.1). Fifty-four (21%) were Catholic, 127 (50%) were Protestant, 3 (1%) were Buddhist, 2 (.8%) were Muslim, 2 (.8%) were atheist, and 9 (4%) were agnostic. Forty-three (17%) indicated that they believed in God but had no specific faith and 15 (6%) indicated that their faith was "other" than those options listed (see Table 1 for more information on the final sample). After death qualification, each cell had an average of 14.3 participants, with cell sizes ranging from 12 to 18 participants.

## Categories of Dependent Variables

Results are categorized according to six categories of dependent variables: CEST measures, verdict confidence, perceptions of responsibility, general feelings of retribution and mercy, factors that influenced decisions and individual differences.

## Scoring and Analyses

Two separate CEST measures were also used as dependent measures (See Appendix F). In the "Linda" problem, individuals processing experientially are more likely than those processing rationally to make conjunction errors (i.e., stating that the probability of two events occurring together is greater than one of the events occurring alone; Epstein, et al., 1992). In this problem, participants are given a priming paragraph that contains a description of a fictitious person named Linda. The description is constructed to be characteristic of an active feminist and uncharacteristic of a bank teller. Participants are then asked to rank eight statements by "the degree to which Linda resembles the typical member of that class." Among the list are: "Linda is a bank teller" and "Linda is a bank teller and is active in the feminist movement" (the conjunction statement).

Individuals processing experientially are more likely than those processing rationally to rank the conjunction as more probable than the single statement that "Linda is a bank teller," although that is logically impossible. Individuals who are processing experientially are more likely to rely on the mental heuristic provided by the priming paragraph and display the conjunction fallacy, whereas individuals processing rationally are more likely to rely on their sense of logic to solve the problem (Epstein, et al., 1992).

If the participant indicated that "Linda is a bank teller" was more likely than "Linda is a bank teller and is active in the feminist movement," the participant was considered to be processing rationally.  On the other hand, if the participant indicated that "Linda is a bank teller" was less likely than "Linda is a bank teller and is active in the feminist movement" (a conjunction error), the participant was considered to be processing experientially.

The other CEST measure was the combination of two questions in which participants were asked to judge the behavior of actors in a short vignette (See Appendix F).  In the first question, participants read a paragraph in which one actor's behavior was an act of commission, and the other actor's behavior was an act of omission (Epstein, et al., 1992).  The participant then indicated which actor was more foolish on a scale of 1 (Actor 1 was more foolish) to 9 (Actor 2 was more foolish) with a midpoint of 5 (Actors were equally foolish).  In the second question, participants read a paragraph in which one actor's behavior was constrained, while the second actor's behavior was unconstrained (Epstein, et al., 1992). Participants were again asked which actor was more foolish, using the same scale as in the first question.

The "rational" answer to both questions is 5 (the actors were equally foolish). If the participant circled 5, they were given a score of "0," indicating that they were rational. If the participant circled 4 or 6, they received a score of "1," indicating that they were 1 unit from being rational. If the participant circled 3 or 7, they received a score of "2" and so on. Thus, the result was a scale of 0 (very rational) to 4 (very experiential). The scores of these two questions were combined to form the CEST scale.

The primary dependent variable was a "verdict confidence" measure constructed from two separate questions.  Participants indicated their verdict (life without the possibility of parole or death) then rated the level of confidence they had in their verdict on a scale from 1 (very uncertain) to 7 (very certain). A verdict of death was scored as –1 and a life sentence was scored as 1. The verdict score and the confidence score were multiplied to create a verdict confidence score that ranged from –7 (indicating that the participant was very confident in a death sentence) to +7 (indicating that the participant was very confident in a life sentence). An analysis of variance was conducted containing case type (high aggravators or high mitigators), appeal (religious, non-religious or control) and directive (Rational, Experiential or control) as independent variables and verdict confidence as a dependent variable. Tukey's HSD was used to perform post-hoc analyses.

Dependent Variable One: CEST Measures

Although the CEST scale and Linda problems were intended to measure the same phenomenon (rational or experiential thinking), they were not correlated ($r = .06$, $p > .05$). As none of the analyses for the Linda problem were significant, discussion of the CEST results will focus on the CEST scale; the "Linda" problem will not be discussed further.

<u>Effects of Processing Directives</u>

It was expected that rational directives would increase rational processing as measured by the CEST tasks. Conversely, receiving a directive to process experientially was expected to increase experiential processing. Recall that the higher the score on the CEST scale, the more experientially the participant was processing. Analyses indicated that directive type had an effect on the CEST scale ($F (2,226) = 3.77$, $p < .05$), however not all of the means were in the expected direction. Tukey's HSD post-hoc analyses indicated that the rational group ($M = 2.90$) did not differ from the experiential group ($M = 2.29$, $p = .22$), but did differ from the control group ($M = 1.88$, $p = .02$). The experiential group did not differ from the control group ($p = .50$). These means indicate that, as predicted, the experiential directive produced more experiential processing than the control group (although not significantly more). Contrary to the hypothesis, however, the rational directive also produced significantly more experiential processing than the control group. Thus, the processing manipulation did not work exactly as intended.

## Effects of Appeals

It was predicted that participants who received religious appeals would process more experientially, whereas participants who did not receive appeals would process more rationally. Non-religious emotional appeals were expected to have similar, yet weaker, effects as religious appeals. Analyses revealed that appeals did not influence rational or experiential processing on the CEST scale ($F_{(2,226)} = .055$, $p > .05$).

## Dependent Variable Two: Verdict Confidence

## Effects of Appeals

It was expected that individuals receiving appeals (either religious or non-religious) would issue more overall death sentences than those not receiving emotional appeals. There was no main effect on the verdict confidence measure ($F_{(2,237)} = .067$, $p > .05$).

## Effects of Directives

While the directives told participants how to make the decision, they did not tell participants which decision (i.e., life in prison or death penalty) to make. Thus, no predictions were made for the main effect of processing directives on the verdict confidence measure, and no effect was found ($F_{(2,237)} = 2.01$, $p > .05$).

## Effects of Case Type

It was expected that individuals reading the trial summary with high aggravators would be more likely to sentence the defendant to death than individuals reading the trial summary with high mitigators. Results supported this hypothesis: Participants in the high aggravator condition ($M = -.12$) scored lower on the verdict confidence measure (indicating that they were more in favor of a death sentence) than participants in the high mitigator condition ($M = 3.05$, $F (2,237) = 20.5$, $p < .001$).

## Interactions

Appeals and processing directives were expected to influence the ability of participants to weigh aggravating and mitigating factors properly. Recall that analyses revealed a main effect of case type on the verdict confidence variable; participants in the high aggravators condition issued more death sentences than participants in the high mitigators condition. This represents proper weighing of aggravators and mitigators. It was expected, however that appeals and experiential directives would interfere with decision-making and rational directives would facilitate decision-making; thus a series of interactions were hypothesized.

_Interaction between appeals and case type_. An interaction was expected between the type of trial summary a participant received (high aggravators or high mitigators) and the type of appeal (religious, non-religious or none). It was expected that participants receiving appeals would be less sensitive to aggravators and mitigators than participants not receiving appeals. This interaction was not significant, however ($F (2,237) = .08$, $p > .05$).

_Interaction between processing directives and case type_. It was expected that participants receiving experiential directives would be less sensitive to aggravators and mitigators than participants receiving either no directive or a rational directive. This expected interaction between processing directive and case type was not significant (F (2,237) = .137, p > .05).

Interaction between processing directives and appeals. It was expected that, for individuals receiving an appeal (either religious or non-religious), those also receiving an experiential directive would issue more death sentences than either participants in the control (no directive) condition or participants in the rational directive condition, who would issue the fewest death sentences. Participants in the no-appeal (control) condition were not expected to be affected by directives. This interaction was not significant (F (4,237) = .446, p > .05).

Three-way interaction of appeal, processing directive and case type. Although the three-way interaction was not expected, it was included in the model. This interaction was significant (F (4,237) = 3.37, p < .05). Analyses indicated that four groups were able to weigh aggravators and mitigators appropriately (i.e., those reading the high aggravators condition gave significantly more death sentences than those reading the high mitigators condition): 1) Non-religious appeal and rational directive; 2) Religious appeal and experiential directive; 3) Religious appeal and no directive; and 4) No-appeal and no-directive. As there does not seem to be any pattern to these results, further research and replication are needed.

## CEST Processing

Scores on the CEST scale were negatively correlated with verdict confidence (r = -.128, p < .05), indicating that the more experientially participants were processing information, the more they were in favor of the death penalty.

Dependent Variable Three: Perception of Responsibility

Participants were asked to rate the level of perceived responsibility that each of six entities (i.e., judge's instructions, the defendant, Biblical authority, juror, victim and chance) had for the sentencing decision. A 3-way MANOVA was conducted with the answers to these six questions as dependent variables.

<u>Effects of Case Type</u>

Case type (high aggravators or high mitigators) was not expected to affect perceptions of responsibility, and analysis confirmed this prediction ($F_{(6,228)} = .64$, $p > .05$).

<u>Effects of Appeals</u>

It was expected that jurors receiving retributive appeals (both religious and non-religious) would feel less personally responsible for the sentencing decision than participants who did not receive appeals. Additionally, participants in the religious appeals group were expected to place greater responsibility for the sentencing decision on Biblical authority as compared to other appeal groups. Contrary to these hypotheses, appeals did not affect the amount of responsibility participants placed on these six variables ($F_{(12,458)} = .65$, $p > .05$).

<u>Effects of Directive</u>

It was expected that receiving a rational directive would increase perceived personal responsibility, while receiving an experiential directive would decrease the amount of perceived responsibility. Additionally, the experiential directive was expected to lead participants to place more blame on others (e.g., Biblical authority or the defendant). These effects were expected to occur for both religious and non-religious appeals. Analyses indicated that directives did not affect responsibility assigned to the variables (F (12,458) = 1.39, p > .05).

<u>Interactions</u>

No interactions were predicted among case type, appeal, and directive, and none were found (Fs < 1.19, ps >.24).

<u>Correlations among Responsibility Questions and CEST Processing</u>

It was also of interest to determine if processing, as measured by the CEST scale, was related to the assignment of responsibility. Correlational analyses revealed that scores on the CEST measure were not related to any of the responsibility questions (all r < .095, p > .14).

Correlational analyses were also conducted among all of the responsibility questions (see Table 2). Results revealed that responsibility assigned to Biblical authority was related to responsibility assigned to several other entities. The more responsibility assigned to "Biblical authority," the less responsibility assigned to the "juror" (r = -.138, p < .05), the less assigned to "judge's instructions/state law" (r = -.140, p < .05), and the more responsibility assigned to "chance" (r = .217, p < .001).

Assigning responsibility to "chance" was also positively related to assigning responsibility to the "defendant" (r = .180, p < .01) and the "victim" (r = .209, p < .01).

Additionally, "judge's instructions/state law" responsibility was negatively correlated with "chance" responsibility (r = -.138, p < .05) and positively correlated with "juror" responsibility (r = .307, p < .001).

"Juror" responsibility was also positively correlated with "victim" responsibility (r = .130, p < .05).

Dependent Variable Four: General Feelings of Retribution and Mercy

A 3-way MANOVA was performed with answers to the four questions regarding retribution and mercy in general (e.g., "Criminals should be shown mercy" and "Murderers deserve the death penalty because they killed") as dependent variables.

<u>Effects of Case Type</u>

No predictions were made for case type (high aggravators or high mitigators), and analyses indicate that case type did not affect feelings of retribution and mercy ($F_{(4,234)} = .23, p > .05$).

<u>Effects of Appeals</u>

It was expected that jurors receiving religious appeals would be more supportive of general notions of retribution and less supportive of forgiveness than participants receiving non-religious appeals, and that both groups receiving appeals would be more supportive of retribution and less supportive of forgiveness than the no-appeal group. Analyses did not support these hypotheses ($F_{(8,470)} = 1.09, p > .05$).

<u>Effects of Directives</u>

Analyses indicated that directives did not influence answers to these statements ($F_{(8,470)} = 1.50, p > .05$).

<u>Interactions</u>

<u>Interaction between case type and appeal</u>. There was a significant interaction between case type and appeal ($F_{(8,470)} = 2.29, p < .05$) that was driven by the responses to

Table 2: Correlations among responsibility questions

| | Judge's instruc- tions/ state law | Biblical authority | Juror | Defendant | Chance | Victim |
|---|---|---|---|---|---|---|
| Judge's instruc- tions/ state law | - | -.140* | .307** | 0.039 | -.138* | -0.033 |
| Biblical authority | -.140* | - | -1.38* | -0.039 | .217** | 0.101 |
| Juror | .307* | -.138* | - | 0.054 | -0.118 | .130* |
| Defendant | 0.039 | -0.039 | 0.054 | - | .180** | 0.011 |
| Chance | -.138* | .217** | -0.118 | .180* | - | .209** |
| Victim | -0.033 | 0.101 | .130* | 0.011 | .209** | - |

* p < .05
* * p < .01

the statements "Criminals should be forgiven for their acts" (F (2, 237) = 3.28, p < .05) and "Criminals should be shown mercy" (F (2, 237) = 6.27, p < .01).

For the "Criminals should be forgiven for their acts" question, the type of appeal did not affect participants who received the trial facts containing high mitigators (Ms = 3.51-3.88; ts <1.07, ps >.29).  In the high aggravators condition, there was no difference between the no-appeal condition (M = 3.10) and the religious appeal condition (M = 3.26; t (86) = .51, p > .05), but the non-religious appeal group (M = 4.04) agreed with this statement significantly more than both the religious appeal (t (89) = 2.19, p < .05) and the no-appeal group (t (85) = 2.49, p < .05).

Similarly, for the "Criminals should be shown mercy" question, the type of appeal did not affect participants who received the trial facts containing high mitigators (Ms = 3.2-3.55; ts <.97, ps >.16). In the high aggravators condition, there was no difference between the no-appeal condition (M = 3.39) and either the religious appeal condition (M = 2.85; t (86) = 1.54, p > .05) or the non-religious condition (M = 3.62; t (85) = .9, p > .05). The non-religious group agreed with this statement significantly more than the religious group, however (t (89) = 2.57, p < .05).

## Correlations among Feelings of Retribution/Mercy Questions and CEST Processing

Correlational analyses revealed a relationship between CEST scores and the participant's feelings about forgiveness and retribution. The higher the score on the CEST measure (indicating more experiential thinking), the less agreement that criminals should be forgiven (r = -.187, p < .01) or shown mercy (r = -.148, p < .05) and more agreement that criminals deserve death (r = .134, p < .05) and "payback" for their crimes (r = .137, p < .05), suggesting that the more experientially a participant scores on the CEST measure, the more supportive they are of retribution and the less mercy they feel.

## Dependent Variable Five: Factors that Influenced Decisions

It was also of interest to determine what factors (e.g., judge's instructions, Biblical authority, prosecutors arguments) participants believed influenced their decisions. Although no specific hypotheses were made, an exploratory analysis was conducted. A 3-way MANOVA was performed with these seven factors as dependent variables.

Effects of Appeals

Appeals did not affect answers to the questions regarding what influenced participants' sentencing decisions (F $(14,464) = .87$, p $> .05$).

Effects of Directives

Directives had a marginal effect on answers (F $(14,464) = 1.67$, p $= .058$). Univariate tests showed ratings of the influence of "evidence" was marginally significant (F $(2, 237) = 2.71$, p $= .069$). Post hoc tests revealed that the rational group (M $= 6.40$) relied more on the evidence than either the experiential group (M $= 5.90$) or the control group (M $= 6.03$), although none of the differences were statistically significant (ps $> .07$).

The effect of directives on ratings of influence of "personal religious beliefs" was also marginally significant (F $(2, 237) = 2.60$, p $= .07$). Post hoc tests revealed that the experiential group was more likely to rely on personal religious beliefs (M $= 3.13$) than the rational group (M $= 2.45$, p $= .04$), but did not differ from the control group (M $= 2.78$, p $> .05$). The rational and control groups also did not differ (p $> .05$).

These patterns suggest that receiving a rational directive led participants to rely somewhat more on the evidence, while receiving an experiential directive led participants to rely more on their personal religious beliefs.

Effects of Case Type

Case type had a significant effect on answers to the "influence" questions (F $(7,231) = 2.72$, p $< .05$). Univariate tests showed this effect was a result of the measure "prosecutor's arguments" (F $(1, 237) = 9.43$, p $< .05$). Participants in the high aggravator case (M $= 4.75$) were more influenced by the prosecutor's arguments than participants in the high mitigator case (M $= 4.15$).

## Interactions

No interactions were predicted among case type, appeal, and directive, and none were found (Fs < 2.29, ps > .05.)

## Correlations among "Influence" Questions and CEST processing

Correlational analyses revealed a negative correlation between CEST and being influenced by judge's instructions (r = -214, p < .01), indicating that the more experientially a participant processed information, the less they were influenced by the instructions. CEST scores did not correlate with any other item on the "influence" list (rs < .11, ps > .08).

Correlational analyses were also performed among the "influence" questions (see Table 3). Results indicated that the more a participant relied on "Biblical authority," the less they relied on "judge's instructions/state law" (r = -.176, p < .01), the less they relied on "evidence presented in the case" (r = -.331, p < .01), and the more they relied on personal religious beliefs (r = .767, p < .01).

In addition to the negative correlation with "Biblical authority," being influenced by "judge's instructions" was negatively correlated with being influenced by "personal religious beliefs" (r = -.221, p < .01) and "personal feelings about the death penalty" (r = -.203, p < .01). "Judge's instructions" was also positively correlated with "evidence presented in the case" (r = .334, p < .01). "Evidence" was also negatively related to "personal religious beliefs" (r = -.371, p < .01), which was correlated with "Personal feelings about the death penalty" (r = .306, p < .01).

Table 3: Correlations among "Influence" questions

|  | Judge's instructions | Biblical authority | Defense arguments | Prosecution arguments | Evidence presented | Personal religious beliefs | Feelings about death penalty |
|---|---|---|---|---|---|---|---|
| Judge's instructions/ state law | - | -.176** | 0.068 | 0.034 | .334** | -.221** | -.203** |
| Biblical authority | -.176** | - | 0.062 | 0.092 | -.331** | .767** | 0.092 |
| Defense attorney arguments | 0.068 | 0.062 | - | .371** | 0.022 | 0.069 | -0.022 |
| Prosecution arguments | 0.034 | 0.092 | .371** | - | 0.104 | 0.064 | 0.076 |
| Evidence presented | .334** | -.331** | 0.022 | 0.104 | - | -.371** | 0.056 |
| Personal religious beliefs | -.221** | .767** | 0.069 | 0.064 | -.371** | - | .306** |
| Feelings about death penalty | -.203** | 0.092 | -0.022 | 0.076 | -0.056 | .306** | - |

** p< .01

## Individual Differences

Individual difference measures were analyzed to measure their associations with the dependent measures. These individual differences include gender, age, fundamentalism, evangelism, devotionalism, literal interpretism, and the REI measure.[4]

### Gender

Since gender is often an important variable in decision-making, all principal analyses were repeated, using gender as a fourth independent variable. Only results that were altered by the addition of gender will be reported below. Except as noted below, gender did not influence the dependent variables.

<u>Verdict confidence</u>. Analyses revealed a main effect for gender ($F$ (1,219) = 10.59, $p < .01$). Males were more in favor of the death penalty (M = -.190) than females (M = 2.11). There was also an unexpected significant main effect for directives ($F$ (2,219) = 3.39, $p < .05$). Individuals receiving experiential directives scored higher on the verdict confidence measure (M = 2.35), indicating that this group was more in favor of life sentences than either the rational directive (M = .963) or the no directive (M = .818) groups. Post-hoc tests revealed that none of these groups were significantly different from one another, however.

The interaction between case type, appeal and directive that was produced by the three-way ANOVA was not significant in the four-way ($F$ (4,219) = 2.39, $p > .05$).

There was an unpredicted three-way interaction between gender, case type and appeal ($F$ (2,219) = 4.22, $p < .05$). Follow-up analyses revealed that males could properly

---

[4] Religious affiliation was also included as an independent measure, however these analyses did not contribute any significant findings. Thus these analyses will not be reported.

weigh aggravators and mitigators in the non-religious appeal condition only, while females could properly weigh aggravators and mitigators in both the religious and control appeal conditions, ts > 2.5, ps < .05. Verdict confidence scores for males in the religious and no-appeal conditions, and for females in the non-religious condition, were not affected by case type, indicating that participants in these groups were unable to weigh aggravators and mitigators properly.

All other results for the verdict confidence measure did not change when gender was added as an independent variable.

CEST measure. On the CEST measure, gender was added as a fourth variable, and ANOVA was performed. Gender did not have a main effect on the CEST measure (F (1,208) = 2.09, p > .05). The main effect of processing directive that was found in the three-way analysis was no longer significant once gender was added as a fourth variable (F (2,208) = 1.78, p > .05). All other results for the CEST measure did not change by adding gender.

Perceived responsibility. For the Perceived Responsibility measures, gender was added as a fourth variable and MANOVA was performed. There was no main effect for gender (F (6,210) = 1.41, p > .05). None of the findings of the three-way MANOVA were changed by adding gender.

General feelings of retribution and mercy. Gender was added as a fourth variable and MANOVA was conducted with the General Feelings of Retribution and Mercy measures. There was no main effect for gender (F (4,216) = .31, p > .05). The interaction between case type and appeal that was found in the three-way MANOVA was no longer significant once gender was added (F (8,434) = 1.62, p > .05). None of the other results changed as a result of adding gender as a fourth variable.

Factors that influenced decisions. Gender was also added as a fourth variable in the MANOVA with the factors that influenced decisions as dependent variables. There was no main effect for gender (F (7,213) = 1.32, p > .05). Directives no longer influenced which factors were influential (F (14,428) = 1.36, p > .05).

In sum, gender had a main effect on verdict confidence: Males were more in favor of death than females. Further, a three-way interaction revealed that males could properly weigh aggravators and mitigators in only the non-religious appeal condition, while females could properly weigh these factors in both the control and religious appeal conditions. Finally, gender did not affect CEST processing, perceived responsibility, feelings of retribution and mercy or factors that influenced decisions.

## Age

Pearson's correlation indicated that age was not related to verdict confidence (r = -.081, p > .05).

## Fundamentalism

Individuals who scored high on the fundamentalism scale were expected to be more likely to vote for the death penalty than those scoring low on the fundamentalism scale. Analyses indicated that there was no correlation between fundamentalism and verdict confidence (r = .041, p > .05).

## Evangelism

It was expected that evangelical individuals would be less likely to vote for the death penalty than those individuals who were not evangelical. A Pearson's correlation conducted between scores on the evangelism scale and verdict confidence was not significant (r = -.043, p > .05).

A second measure of evangelism (a "yes" or "no" answer to the question "Have you ever tried to encourage someone to believe in Jesus Christ or to accept Jesus Christ

as his or her savior?") also did not affect verdict confidence
(t (249) = 1.02, p > .05).

## Devotionalism

Although it was expected that the more devotional
individuals were, the less likely they would be to sentence
the defendant to death, the devotionalism scale was not
correlated with verdict confidence (r = .01, p > .05).  An
interaction between case type and the devotionalism scale
was also predicted. It was expected that the greater amount
of time a participant spent engaged in religious activities,
the more influential religious appeals would be on the
participant's decision-making.  Participants were grouped
as "low" or "high" in devotionalism based on a median
split.  A four-way ANOVA was performed, with case type,
directive, appeals and devotionalism as independent
variables and verdict confidence as the dependent variable.
Contrary to the hypothesis, there was no main effect for
appeal (F (2,214) = .78, p > .05) or devotionalism (F
(1,214) = .18, p > .05); nor were there any interactions
between the devotionalism scale and the other variables (Fs
< 1.93, ps > .15). Similarly, the single devotionalism item
was not correlated with verdict confidence (r = .044, p >
.05).

## Literal Interpretism

It was predicted that those who felt the Bible should be
interpreted literally (i.e., a "yes" answer to the question
"Do you believe that the Bible is the actual word of God
and is to be taken literally, word for word?") would be
more likely to support the death penalty than those
individuals who did not believe in a strict translation. As
hypothesized, literal interpreters scored lower on the
verdict confidence measure (M = .400) and thus were more
likely to sentence the defendant to death, than participants
who were not literal interpreters (M = 1.89, t (249) = 2.01,
p < .05).

## CEST Processing Style

The Rational-Experiential Inventory (REI) is composed of two sub-scales: The Need for Cognition scale (NFC) which measures rational thinking, and the Faith in Intuition scale (FI) which measures experiential thinking. These scales measure the participant's processing style as a general trait (e.g., if the participant generally tends to process experientially or rationally in every day life) rather than measuring the processing style being used at the time of the survey. It was hypothesized that individuals scoring high on the NFC scale would be more "rational" on the CEST measure and individuals scoring high on the FI scale would be more "experiential" on the CEST measure. Analyses revealed that CEST scores were not related to scores on the NFC scale ($r = .008$, $p > .05$) or the FI scale ($r = .004$, $p > .05$). Further, the NFC and FI scores were not correlated ($r = .11$, $p > .05$).

<u>Verdict confidence</u>. Participants were separated into either a "high NFC" or "low NFC" group and either a "low FI" or "high FI" group according to median splits. A five-way ANOVA was conducted with case type, appeal, directive, NFC, and FI as independent variables and verdict confidence as the dependent variable.

There were no main effects for appeals, directives, NFC, or FI ($Fs < 2.20$, $ps > .113$). However, consistent with the principal analysis reported above, there was a main effect for case type ($F (1,177) = 25.92$, $p < .001$). Participants who read the case facts that were high in aggravators ($M = -.23$) were more in favor of the death penalty than those reading case facts high in mitigators ($M = 3.08$).

Although it was expected that participants scoring high in rational processing on the NFC scale would be better able to weigh aggravators and mitigators than those low in rational processing, there was no interaction between case type and NFC ($F (1,177) = .04$, $p > .05$). Similarly it was expected that those scoring low in experiential processing on the FI scale would be better able to weigh aggravators and mitigators than those scoring high in experiential processing; however, there was not a significant interaction between case type and FI ($F_{(1,177)} = 2.39$, $p > .05$).

There was a three-way interaction between case type, appeal, and NFC ($F_{(1,177)} = 6.79$, $p < .001$). Follow up analyses indicated that only two groups could properly weigh aggravators and mitigators: The religious appeal, low NFC group ($t_{(34)} = 3.2$, $p < .01$) and the no-appeal, high NFC group ($t_{(43)} = 3.9$, $p < .001$). The no-appeal, high NFC group would be expected to weigh aggravators and mitigators properly, as they are rational thinkers who are not influenced by emotional appeals. However, it is surprising that the religious appeal, low NFC group would also be able to weigh properly, as participants in this group are less rational thinkers who experienced an emotional religious appeal.

There was an uninterpretable three-way interaction between directive, appeal, and NFC ($F_{(1,177)} = 2.54$, $p < .05$) and an unpredicted four-way interaction between case type, directive, appeal, and NFC ($F_{(1,177)} = 2.82$, $p < .05$). There was also an unexpected four-way interaction between case type, directive, appeal, and FI ($F_{(1,177)} = 3.31$, $p < .05$). These four-way interactions were not interpretable and may not be reliable, as some of the groups had as few as four participants.

Relationship between REI and responsibility questions. Correlational analyses were performed among the NFC and FI scales and the questions regarding which entities the participant felt were responsible for the sentencing decision. Scores on the NFC scale were positively related to finding the "judge's instructions/state law" responsible ($r = .16$, $p < .05$) and "juror responsible" ($r = .137$, $p < .05$). NFC scores were negatively related to "victim responsible" ($r = -.174$, $p < .01$). Scores on the NFC scale did not correlate with any of the other responsibility questions (all $rs < .125$, $ps > .05$).

Scores on the FI scale correlated with "judge's instructions/state law responsible" ($r = .222$, $p < .001$), indicating that the more experiential participants were on the FI scale, the more responsibility they placed on the judge or state law. Scores on the FI scale did not correlate with any other responsibility measures (all rs< .06, ps > .37).

Relationship between REI and attitudes about mercy and retribution. Correlational analyses among NFC scores and the questions regarding mercy and retribution were not significant (all rs< .11, ps > .08). The only question correlated with FI scores was "criminals deserve 'payback' for their crimes" ($r = .130$, $p < .05$), indicating that the more experiential a participant was on the FI scale, the more they agreed with this statement. The other questions were not significantly related to the FI scale (all rs< .12, ps > .07).

Relationship between REI and factors rated as influential. Additional analyses were conducted to investigate relationships between the REI scales and the questions regarding factors that were influential to the participant's sentencing decision. Scores on the NFC scale were negatively correlated with "Biblical authority" ($r = -.172$, $p < .01$), indicating that the more rational participants were on the NFC scale, the less they relied on Biblical authority. NFC scores were positively related to being influenced by "evidence presented" ($r = .164$, $p < .05$), indicating that the higher they scored on the NFC scale, the more they relied on the evidence. No other questions on the NFC scale or the FI scale correlated with any influence measures (all rs< .12, ps > .06).

Summary of Individual Difference Measures

Gender and literal interpretism were the only individual difference measures that affected verdict confidence.

Females were less likely to issue death sentence than males. Additionally, males could properly weigh aggravators and mitigators only in the non-religious appeal condition, while females could properly weigh these factors in both control and religious appeal conditions. Literal interpreters were more likely to sentence the defendant to death than participants who were not literal interpreters. Verdict confidence was not related to age, fundamentalism, evangelism, devotionalism, NFC scores or FI scores. The absence of interactions indicates that devotionalism, FI and NFC failed to affect participants' ability to weigh aggravators and mitigators.

CEST scores were not related to scores on either the NFC or FI scales. Although it could be expected that people with high FI scores (indicating high experiential processing) would do worse on the CEST measure than those with low FI scores, this was not the case. Similarly, it was expected that participants scoring high on the NFC scale (indicating high rational processing) would perform better on the CEST measure than those scoring low on the NFC scale, however the measures were not related.

The perception of responsibility measures were not affected by gender, but responsibility placed on "judge's instructions/state law" was positively related to scores on both the FI and NFC scales. In addition, finding the "juror responsible" was positively related to NFC scores, and finding the "victim" responsible was negatively correlated with NFC scores.

Neither gender nor NFC scores correlated with the retribution and mercy items, and FI only correlated with "criminals deserve 'payback,'" indicating that the more experientially the individual was on the FI scale, the more they agreed with that statement.

Statements about what influenced the sentencing decision were unaffected by gender or scores on the FI scale. Scores on the NFC scale were negatively correlated with being influenced by "Biblical authority" and positively related to "evidence" indicating that the more rational the score on the NFC, the less reliance on the Bible and the more reliance on the evidence.

## DISCUSSION

### CEST Processing

It was expected that rational directives would produce rational processing, and experiential directives would lead to experiential processing as measured on the CEST scale. Instead, results indicated that receiving either type of directive increased experiential processing. In fact, rational directives led to the highest level of experiential thinking of all the groups. It is uncertain why this result would occur. Appeals also did not affect processing type as measured on the CEST scale. This suggests that appeals, at least as operationalized here, did not affect processing type, perhaps because the appeals were not strong enough to lead to experiential processing.

### Verdict Confidence

Contrary to hypotheses, neither appeals nor directives affected verdict confidence scores. Case type affected verdict confidence in the predicted direction: Participants reading a case containing high aggravators scored lower (indicating they were more in favor of death) than those reading the high mitigators case type. None of the expected interactions were found. This indicates that appeals and directives did not affect the ability to weigh aggravators and mitigators properly. A three-way interaction was found, but is not interpretable according to the hypotheses. This initial study supports the conclusion that religious appeals do not affect jurors' sentencing decision.

A significant correlation was found between verdict confidence and the CEST scale, indicating that the more experientially participants were processing, the more they were in favor of the death penalty. This finding is an indication that, despite the absence of any direct effects of the appeal and directive manipulations on participants' verdicts, how individuals process information does have some important consequences on their decision-making as jurors.

Perceptions of Responsibility

Perceptions of responsibility for the sentencing decision were not affected by case type, appeals, directives, or CEST scores. There were some significant correlations among the responsibility questions, however. Responsibility assigned to Biblical authority was negatively related to responsibility assigned to jurors. Thus, the more responsibility an individual placed on the Bible, the less personal responsibility s/he accepted as a juror. These results have implications for the legal system, as courts have indicated that sentences are not valid if jurors believe that the responsibility for the sentence rests elsewhere (*Caldwell v. Mississippi*, 1985). Future studies should further investigate the relationship between perceptions of responsibility and Biblical authority.

General Feelings of Retribution and Mercy

There were no main effects of case type, appeals or directives on the retribution and mercy items; however, there was an interaction between case type and appeals on the two mercy items. There were no differences among the three appeal groups in the high mitigators condition. However in the high aggravators condition, receiving a non-religions appeal led to greater support for mercy. For both mercy questions, those in the high aggravators/ non-religious appeal condition had the most positive notions of mercy of any group. It is not clear why a more severe case containing a non-religious retributive appeal would lead to greater feelings of mercy.

These retribution and mercy items were also related to the CEST processing measure. The more experientially a participant was processing, the less forgiving and merciful the person felt, and the more s/he felt that the criminal deserved death and payback. These findings are consistent with the positive relationship between experiential processing and sentencing the defendant to death.

Factors that Influenced Decisions

While appeals did not affect answers to the "influence" questions, case type did affect these items: Participants in the high aggravators condition were more influenced by the prosecutor's arguments than participants in the high mitigators condition. It is possible that participants form ideas of what should happen to the defendant as they read about the trial. Then, when the attorneys deliver their closing arguments, participants compare the arguments to these ideas in their head. The closer the agreement between the attorney's argument and their perceptions of the case, the more participants feel influenced by the argument. Thus, when receiving a high aggravator case type, a participant may feel that the defendant deserves death, an idea that fits well with the prosecutor's arguments, leading to the feeling of being very influenced by the prosecutor's arguments. This explanation comports with the "story model" of juror decision-making, which suggests that when jurors are sentencing a defendant, they often rely on a "story" summary that they have constructed to explain the evidence (Pennington & Hastie, 1986; 1988).

Additionally, receiving a rational directive led participants to report relying more on the evidence, while receiving an experiential directive led participants to report relying more on personal religious beliefs. These results are consistent with the notions that rational directives lead to decisions based on logic, while experiential directives lead to decisions based on emotions (Epstein, 1990, Epstein, 1994, Epstein, et. al., 1992).

CEST analysis revealed that the more an individual was processing experientially, the less s/he relied on the judge's instructions/state law. Additionally, the more participants relied on Biblical authority, the less they relied on judge's instructions/state law or evidence, and the more they relied on personal religious beliefs. Conversely, the more participants relied on judges instructions, the more they relied evidence, and the less they relied on personal religious beliefs and personal feelings about death penalty.

It is somewhat disturbing that the more a participant relied on the Bible, the less s/he relied on evidence and judge's instructions. This finding lends some support to the notion that Biblical appeals improperly affect jurors, since Biblical influence leads to less reliance on the evidence and instructions. As this influence did not extend to the effects on verdicts, more research is necessary to fully determine the effects of religion on jury decision-making.

Individual Differences

While age and religious affiliation were not related to verdict confidence, other individual differences, such as gender and scores on the literal interpretism scale, were associated with verdicts.

<u>Gender</u>

Gender had a main affect on verdict confidence, with males indicating that they were more in favor of a death sentence than females. This finding comports with findings from previous studies (Sandys & McGarrell, 1995; Whitehead & Blankenship, 2000). An interaction with appeals indicated that males could properly weigh aggravators and mitigators only in the non-religious appeal condition, while females could properly weigh these factors in both the control and religious appeal conditions. Gender did not affect CEST processing, perceived responsibility, feelings of retribution and mercy or factors that influenced decisions. Adding gender to the other analyses did not greatly affect the overall pattern of findings.

<u>Religious scales</u>

There was no relationship between verdict confidence and fundamentalism, evangelism, or devotionalism. These findings are counter to a study which found that those scoring high on the fundamentalism scale were more likely to support the death penalty, and those who were more devotional or evangelical were less in support of the death penalty (Young, 1992). The discrepancy between the Young study and the current study could be due to the samples used. Young used survey data which involved a much broader sample than the current study. As the current study used mostly white students from a mid-western university, the range of responses on the religious measures could be restricted, limiting the findings on the religious measures

The literal interpretism measure was related to scores on the verdict confidence scale; individuals who believed in a literal interpretation of the Bible were more likely to sentence the defendant to death than those who did not have that belief. This finding replicates two other studies which found a positive relationship between belief in a strict interpretation of the Bible and support for the death penalty (Leiber & Woodrick, 1997; Young, 1992).

<u>Rational-Experiental Inventory (REI)</u>

Although it could be expected that processing experientially (i.e., a higher score on the FI scale) would lead to worse scores on the CEST measure, and processing rationally (i.e., a higher score on the NFC scale) would lead to better scores on the CEST measure, this was not the case. There were no significant relationships between the CEST measure and either FI or NFC scores, a finding that does not support the conclusions of previous studies regarding REI and processing style (Epstein et al., 1996). For example, this previous study reported that high FI scores were associated with a greater reliance on heuristics, rather than logic (Epstein et al., 1996).

Neither NFC nor FI predicted verdict confidence scores. Further, the absence of interactions with case type indicated that neither FI nor NFC affected participants' ability to weigh aggravators and mitigators. Thus, although the participants differed in their processing style, this did not affect their ultimate job of sentencing the defendant. Processing type did, however, relate to some of the other dependent measures. Rational thinkers (i.e., those with high scores on the NFC scale) placed more responsibility on the jurors and judge's instructions/state law, and less responsibility on the victim. Further, rational thinkers were influenced more by the evidence and less by Biblical authority. These results support the general notion that participants who are high in NFC make decisions in ways consistent with those of a "rational" juror (e.g., not blaming the victim, relying on the evidence and not extralegal sources such as the Bible).

CONCLUSION

In sum, the key finding of Study One was that retributive appeals did not seem to have any affect on verdict confidence or the weighing of aggravators and mitigators. Thus, the concerns raised by various courts that religious appeals interfere with jury decision-making seem to be unfounded.

Another concern that has been expressed by various courts is that appeals will lead jurors to feel less personal responsibility for the sentencing decision. While appeals did not affect the amount of responsibility participants assigned to themselves as jurors, there was a negative correlation between placing responsibility on Biblical authority and personal responsibility. These mixed findings indicate that further research is needed to determine if religious appeals improperly affect perceptions of personal responsibility.

Results also indicated that neither retributive appeals nor directives affected processing type. One possible explanation for the failure to find the predicted effects for appeals and directives could simply be because these manipulations were not salient to participants. Thus, Study Two included manipulation check questions to rule out this possibility. The other, more central purpose of Study Two was to investigate whether mercy appeals have the same effects (or lack thereof) as the retributive appeals used in Study One.

# CHAPTER 10

# Study Two: Use of Religious Appeals by Defense Attorneys

Study Two was identical to Study One, except that instead of studying retributive appeals, Study Two investigated the effects of mercy appeals used by defense attorneys. The study was designed to determine whether religious mercy appeals, as well as non-religious mercy appeals, lead to experiential processing, a reduction in sensitivity to aggravators and mitigators, and a diminished sense of responsibility for the sentencing decision. Additionally, this study was intended to determine if the addition of an argument instructing jurors to process rationally can attenuate the effect of emotional appeals, and if individual differences are associated with differences in jurors' decision-making. Study Two manipulated the case facts (high aggravators or high mitigators), the mercy appeal used (religious, non-religious, or none), and the type of processing directives (rational, experiential, or none).

The procedure, dependent measure survey and CEST measure used in Study Two were identical to those used in Study One. The only difference between the studies was the type of appeal used in the closing argument. Whereas the trial summary in Study One contained a retributive appeal by the prosecutor, the trial summary in Study Two contained a mercy appeal from the defense attorney in order to determine if defense appeals have the same effects as prosecutorial appeals.

## HYPOTHESES FOR STUDY TWO

The hypotheses for Study Two will be arranged by independent variable: Emotional appeals, processing directives, case type, and individual differences.

Independent Variable One: Appeals

<u>CEST Dependent Measures</u>

Because mercy appeals (both religious and non-religious) are emotional in nature, they are expected to lead to experiential processing, in a similar manner to retribution appeals. Participants who receive religious appeals are expected to process more experientially, whereas participants who do not receive appeals are expected to process more rationally. The mode of processing will be measured by traditional CEST measures such as the "Linda" problem. Non-religious appeals are expected to have similar, yet weaker, effects as religious appeals.

<u>Verdicts</u>

Johnson (1985) found that participant mock jurors were more punitive towards defendants who used religion as evidence that they should receive a lighter sentence than defendants who did not use religion as evidence. Based on these findings, it is expected that participants in the religious appeals condition will be more likely to issue a death sentence than participants in both the no-appeal condition and the non-religious appeal condition. Participants in the non-religious appeal condition will be the least likely to issue a death sentence.

## Perceived Responsibility

It is hypothesized that religious mercy appeals will lead to reduced perceived personal responsibility, as compared to the no-appeal group. Non-religious mercy appeals are also expected to reduce perceived personal responsibility, however to a lesser degree than religious appeals.

## General Feelings of Retribution and Mercy

It is expected that jurors receiving religious mercy appeals will be more supportive of retribution or "pay back," and less supportive of mercy than participants receiving non-religious mercy appeals or no appeals. Participants receiving non-religious mercy appeals should be the least supportive of retribution and most supportive of mercy of all three groups. This pattern is expected because participants are expected to see a religious defense as unacceptable and thus use it against the defendant, in a similar manner as participants in the Johnson (1985) study.

Independent Variable Two: Processing Directives

## CEST Dependent Measures

In light of the null findings for the directive manipulations in Study One, the hypotheses for Study Two are tentative. Although the directives used in Study One were lengthened for Study Two, it is possible that even the stronger Study Two manipulations will not produce the hypothesized results. Nevertheless, rational directives (e.g., "Make the sentencing decision by closely following the jury instructions") should increase rational processing and reduce experiential processing as measured by the CEST task. Conversely, receiving a directive to process experientially (e.g., "Make the sentencing decisions using your gut feelings") will reduce rational processing and increase experiential processing.

## Verdicts

No predictions are made for the main effect of processing directions on verdicts. The main effect will be qualified by an interaction with religious appeals, described below.

## Perception of Personal Responsibility

It is expected that receiving a rational directive will increase perceived personal responsibility, while receiving an experiential directive will decrease the amount of perceived responsibility. The rational directive emphasizes the importance of following the jury directives, which note that the responsibility for sentencing lies with the jurors. On the other hand, the experiential directive encourages jurors to follow their emotions, which may lead them to blame others (e.g., the judge or the defendant) for the decision.

## Independent Variable Three: Case Type

This manipulation was not expected to affect any of the dependent measures except verdict.

## Verdict

As in Study 1, it is expected that individuals reading the trial summary with high aggravators will be more likely to vote for the death penalty than individuals reading the trial summary with high mitigators.

## Interactions between Independent Variables

## Interaction between Appeals and Case Type

Paralleling Study One, participants receiving a mercy appeal (religious or non-religious) will be less sensitive to the case type manipulation due to their more experiential processing. Participants who do not receive any appeal will be more sensitive to aggravators and mitigators in that they will be more likely to issue a death sentence if they receive the high aggravators case summary than if they receive the high mitigators case summary.

## Interaction between Processing Directives and Case Type

Experiential processing directives are expected to increase experiential processing in the same manner as religious appeals. Thus, the predictions for this interaction parallel those for the interaction between appeals and case type. This hypotheses is made with reservations since this same interaction was expected, but not found, in Study One.

## Interaction between Processing Directives and Appeals

It is expected that individuals in the no-appeal (control) condition will not be affected by directives, but that directives will affect participants in the two appeal conditions. Participants in the religious appeal condition will issue the most death sentences when they receive an experiential instruction, and the least when they receive a rational instruction.  This is expected because of the previous study that found that religious evidence introduced by the defense led to more severe sentences (Johnson, 1985). When encouraged to think experientially, participants will be more likely to rely on their emotions, leading to a more punitive effect, similar to that found in the Johnson study.

This pattern should reverse for non-religious appeals; participants in this group will issue the most death sentences in the rational directive condition and the least when they receive an experiential condition. When encouraged to process experientially, participants in the non-religious condition should be more persuaded by the mercy appeal than if they are encouraged to process rationally. Thus, a non-religious mercy appeal and an experiential directive should lead to the fewest death sentences in this interaction.

### Three-way interaction of Appeal, Processing Directive and Case Type

Although the three-way interaction will be included in the model, no predictions are made for this interaction.

### Individual Differences as Independent Variables

The hypotheses for the individual difference measures are generally the same for those made in Study One, except for the literal interpretism measure, discussed below. Because Study One found differences only on the gender and literal interpretism measures, the hypotheses for the other measures are tentative.

Young (1992) found that literal interpreters (i.e. individuals who believed in a strict translation of the Bible) were more likely to support the death penalty compared to those without that belief. However, that study did not specifically test religious mercy appeals as Study Two proposes. It is expected that these individuals will also be influenced by mercy appeals because they will translate the Bible's instructions for mercy literally.

### METHOD

### Participants

Participants were 351 undergraduate students recruited from the University of Nebraska-Lincoln who received extra credit in their psychology course for their participation and 75 community participants who received $10 for their participation. Community participants were recruited through posters displayed around the community and from local volunteer organizations and community groups.

The total sample consisted of 426 participants (170 males and 251 females) with a mean age of 25.5 years (SD

= 14.8 years). The demographic characteristics of the participants are contained in Table 4. The community and student participants did not differ in race ($X^2$ (5) = 1.44, p > .05), verdict ($X^2$ (1) = 2.56, p > .05) or death qualification ($X^2$ (1) = .57, p > .05). The groups were also similar in scores on the fundamentalism scale (t (417) = .538, p > .05), and the evangelism scale (t (418) = .299, p > .05).

Not surprisingly, the community group was significantly older (M = 52.87 years) than the student group (M = 20.12 years, t (416) = 29.26, p < .05). The groups also differed in gender ($X^2$ (1) = .02, p < .05), with students more likely to be male (43%) than non-students (28%). The groups also differed in religious background ($X^2$ (9) = 22.23, p < .05), as non-students were more likely to be Protestant (73%) and less likely to be Catholic (11%), as compared to students, who were 44% Protestant and 28% Catholic. Non-students (M = 31.26) also scored higher on the devotionalism scale than students (M = 28.55; t (417) = 2.36, p < .05). These differences were not believed to be major differences however, so the groups were combined for further analyses.

Design

The design was a 2 (case facts: High aggravators/high mitigators) X 3 (mercy appeal: Religious/non-religious/control) X 3 (processing directive: Experiential/rational/control) between-participants design. Materials

<u>Death Qualification Questionnaire</u>

As in Study One, participants were death qualified based on the standard established in *Wainwright v. Witt* (1985).

## Trial Summary

The written trial summary was identical to that used in Study One, except that the closing arguments were adapted to accommodate the change from the retributive appeal used in Study One to the mercy appeal used in Study Two. In Study Two, the defense attorney's closing argument (see Appendix B) contained a religious appeal (e.g., "The Bible teaches us mercy and forgiveness"), a non-religious appeal (e.g., "The law allows us to show mercy and forgiveness"), or no appeal (control condition).

The directives contained in the closing argument for Study Two were identical to those in Study One except that the directive was given by the defense attorney instead of the prosecuting attorney.

## Instructions and Verdict Form

The instructions and verdict form were identical to those in Study One.

## Dependent Measures Survey

The dependent measures survey was identical to that used in Study One, with the addition of a series of manipulation check questions designed to test the participants' memories of the appeals (five questions) and directives (four questions) used in the closing arguments. These questions were added because of the possibility that the independent variables did not have the predicted effects in Study One because of manipulation failure.

Additionally, five questions were added to the section measuring the factors that influenced the participants' decisions (e.g., "My feelings about this case," "Logic and reason"; see Appendix E). These questions were intended to measure whether these items influenced their decisions as a result of the directive given. For example, it was expected that participants receiving a rational directive

## Table 4: Comparison of Students and Non-Students

| | | Students (N=351) | Non-Students (N=75) | Overall (N=426) | Final Sample (N= 329) |
|---|---|---|---|---|---|
| Verdict | Life | 75.40% | 84% | 76.90% | 75% |
| Gender* | Male | 43% | 28% | 40.40% | 43% |
| Age* | Mean | 20.12 | 52.87 | 25.5 | 25.48 |
| | Median | 19 | 53 | 19 | 20 |
| | SD | 4.11 | 18.8 | 14.8 | 14.8 |
| Racial/ ethnic background | White | 87% | 91% | 88% | 89% |
| | Black | 2% | - | 2% | 2% |
| | Asian | 4% | 4% | 4% | 4% |
| | Hispanic | 2% | 1% | 2% | 1% |
| | Native American | 1% | 2% | 1% | 1% |
| | Other | 3% | 1% | 3% | 3% |
| Religious Affiliation* | Catholic | 28% | 11% | 25% | 23% |
| | Protestant | 44% | 73% | 50% | 50% |
| | Other | 5% | 4% | 5% | 6% |
| | No specific faith | 13% | 8% | 12% | 13% |
| | Atheist/ Agnostic | 5% | 3% | 5% | 5% |
| Religious Scale Means | Fundamentalism | 30.57 | 29.96 | 30.46 | 30.33 |
| | Evangelism | 24.08 | 24.39 | 24.14 | 23.58 |
| | Devotionalism | 28.55 | 31.26 | 29.02 | 28.45 |
| Death Qualification | Eliminated | 16% | 12% | 15.20% | N/A |

*Students and non-students differed on this measure; p < .05

would agree that "logic and reason" influenced their decisions more than participants receiving an experiential directive.

Procedure

In a manner identical to that of Study One, participants completed the survey either in person, or received the survey through email.

<u>Email versus in person surveys</u>

Some participants completed the survey in person ($N$ = 382), while others were sent an email containing a copy of the survey, which they completed and returned ($N$ = 14). The email and in-person groups did not differ in gender ($X^2$ (1) = 2.64, p > .05), race ($X^2$ (5) = 3.36, p > .05), religious background ($X^2$ (9) = 8.7, p > .05), or verdict ($X^2$ (1) = 3.02, p > .05). Further, there was no difference in the number of participants who were eliminated for death qualification ($X^2$ (1) = 2.64, p > .05). The groups did not differ in scores on the devotionalism scale (t (392) = 1.12, p > .05), the evangelism scale (t (394) = 1.39, p > .05), or the fundamentalism scale (t (392) = 1.57, p > .05), nor did they differ in age (t (391) = 1.5, p > .05). Since email and in-person did not differ in these ways, the groups were combined for further analyses.

RESULTS

Death Qualification

Participants were death-qualified using the Witt death qualification question. Sixteen percent of the sample (n = 69) indicated that their attitudes toward the death penalty were so strong that they would seriously affect them so as to interfere with their performance as a juror. These participants were excluded from the final sample.

## Manipulation Checks

Study Two included a number of manipulation check questions designed to identify participants' ability to recall the content of the religious appeal and directive manipulations. There were five questions concerning the religious appeal manipulation (e.g., "Did the defense attorney give you Biblical examples of why you should forgive the defendant?") and four questions concerning the directive manipulation. The participants were asked "How did the defense attorney tell you to make the sentencing decision?" and were asked to check any or all of the four options that applied (e.g., "Use your gut instincts and feelings"). Participants were eliminated if they gave incorrect answers to three or more of the religious appeal questions or three or more of the directive questions. Application of these criteria eliminated 28 total participants (an additional two participants were eliminated because they did not answer these questions).

The final sample consisted of 329 participants (43% male) with ages ranging from 18-86 (mean age 25.5, SD= 14.8). Seventy-five (23%) were Catholic, 167 (51%) were Protestant, 7 (2%) were Buddhist, 1 was Jewish (.3%), 1 was Hindu (.3%), 1 was Muslim (.3%), 8 (2%) were atheist, and 9 (3%) were agnostic. Forty-one (13%) indicated that they believed in God but had no specific faith and 19 (6%) indicated that their faith was "other" than those options listed. See Table 4 for more information on the final sample. After death qualification, each cell had an average of 18.3 participants with cell sizes ranging from 14 to 24 participants.

## Categories of Dependent Variables

Results will be categorized according to six categories of dependent variables: CEST measures, verdict confidence, perceptions of responsibility, general feelings of retribution and mercy, factors that influenced decisions and individual differences.

Scoring and Analyses

The verdict confidence measure and CEST measures (e.g., "Linda problem") used in Study One were used in Study Two. The analyses (e.g., ANOVAs and MANOVAs) for Study Two were identical to those of Study One.

Dependent Variable One: CEST Measures

The CEST scale and Linda problems are designed to measure the same phenomenon (rational or experiential thinking). Unlike in Study 1, a Pearson Correlation revealed that they were positively correlated ($r = .14$, $p = .02$), indicating that the more experiential a participant scored on the Linda problem, the more experiential the participant scored on the CEST measure.

Effects of Processing Directives

It was expected that rational directives would increase rational processing and reduce experiential processing as measured by the CEST tasks. Conversely, receiving a directive to process experientially would reduce rational processing and increase experiential processing. Analyses indicate that processing directives did not affect scores on the Linda problem ($F$ $(2,299) = 1.54$, $p > .05$) or on the CEST scale ($F$ $(2,296) = 2.56$, $p > .05$).

Effects of Appeals

It was predicted that participants who received religious appeals would process more experientially, whereas participants who did not receive appeals would process more rationally. Non-religious emotional appeals were expected to have similar, yet weaker, effects as religious appeals. Analyses revealed that appeals did not influence rational or experiential thinking on the Linda problem ($F$

(2,299) = .09, p > .05) or the CEST scale (F (2,323) = 1.19, p > .05).

<u>Effects of Case Type</u>

An unexpected effect was found for case type on the CEST measure (F (2,296) = 7.69, p < .01). Participants who received the case facts with high aggravators were more experiential (M = 2.55) than those who read the case containing high mitigators (M = 1.92). Case type did not affect scores on the Linda problem (F (2,299) = 1.57, p > .21).

<u>Interaction</u>

<u>Interaction between case type and directive</u>. There was an unexpected interaction between the case type and directive on the Linda problem (F (2,299) = 4.57, p < .05). Post-hoc tests revealed that, in the high aggravators group, directive did not affect Linda problem scores; however, in the high mitigators group, the no-directive group (M = .75) was significantly more rational than either the experiential group (M = .93, p = .03) or the rational group (M = .91, p = .28). The rational and experiential group did not differ (p = .96). This result indicates that, for the high mitigators group only, receiving either a rational or experiential appeal led participants to be more experiential than not receiving any appeal.

Dependent Variable Two: Verdict Confidence

<u>Effects of Appeals</u>

It was expected that individuals receiving religious appeals would issue more overall death sentences than those not receiving appeals or those receiving a non-religious appeal, who would issue the fewest death sentences. Contrary to the hypothesis, there was no main effect on the verdict confidence measure (F $(2,303)$ = .339, p > .05).

## Effects of Directives

While the directives told participants how to make the decision, they did not tell participants which decision (i.e., life in prison or death penalty) to make.  Thus, no predictions were made for the main effect of processing directives on the verdict confidence measure and no effect was found (F $(2,303)$ = .101, p > .05).

## Effects of Case Type

It was expected that individuals reading the trial summary with high aggravators would be more likely to sentence the defendant to death than individuals reading the trial summary with high mitigators.  Anova indicated that participants in the high aggravator condition (M = 1.59) scored lower on the verdict confidence measure, suggesting that they were more in favor of a death sentence than participants in the high mitigator condition (M = 4.07, F $(2,303)$ = 18.42, p < .001).

## Interactions

Appeals and processing directives were expected to interact with case type, influencing the ability of participants to properly weigh aggravating and mitigating factors.  An interaction between appeals and directives was also expected.

<u>Interaction between appeals and case type</u>.  An interaction was expected between the type of trial summary a participant received (high aggravators or high mitigators) and the type of appeal (religious, non-religious or none).  It was expected that participants receiving appeals would be less sensitive to aggravators and mitigators than participants not receiving appeals. This interaction was not significant, however (F $(2,303)$ = .47, p > .05).

<u>Interaction between processing directives and case type</u>. It was expected that participants receiving experiential appeals would be less sensitive to aggravators and mitigators than participants receiving either no directive or a rational directive. This expected interaction between processing directive and case type was not significant ($F$ $(2,303) = .50$, $p > .05$).

<u>Interaction between processing directives and appeals</u>. It was expected that, for individuals receiving an appeal (either religious or non-religious), those also receiving an experiential directive would issue more death sentences than either participants in the control (no directive) condition or participants in the rational directive condition, who would issue the fewest death sentences. Participants in the no-appeal (control) condition were not expected to be affected by directives. This interaction was not significant ($F$ $(4,303) = 1.40$, $p > .05$).

<u>CEST Processing</u>

Scores on the verdict confidence scale were not correlated with CEST scores ($r = -.039$, $p > .05$), or answers to the Linda problem ($r = .06$, $p > .5$).

Dependent Variable Three: Perception of Responsibility

Participants were asked to rate the level of perceived responsibility that each of six entities (i.e., judge's instructions, the defendant, Biblical authority, juror, victim and chance) had for the sentencing decision. A 3-way MANOVA was conducted with the answers to these six questions as dependent variables.

### Effects of Case Type

Case type (high aggravators or high mitigators) was not expected to affect perceptions of responsibility, and analyses revealed that it did not (F (6,302) = 1.50, p > .05).

### Effects of Appeals

It was expected that jurors receiving mercy appeals (both religious and non-religious) would feel less personally responsible for the sentencing decision than participants who did not receive appeals. Contrary to the hypotheses, appeals did not affect the amount of responsibility participants placed on these six variables (F (12,606) = 1.34, p > .05).

### Effects of Directives

It was expected that receiving a rational directive would increase perceived personal responsibility, while receiving an experiential directive would decrease the amount of perceived responsibility. Additionally, the experiential directive was expected to lead participants to place more blame on others (e.g., Biblical authority or the defendant). Analyses indicated that directives did not affect responsibility assigned to the variables (F (12,606) = .65, p > .05).

### Interactions

No interactions were predicted among case type, appeal, and directive, and none were found (Fs < 1.35, ps > .05.)

### Correlations among Responsibility Questions and CEST Processing

It was also of interest to determine if processing, as measured by CEST, affected the assignment of responsibility. Correlational analyses revealed that scores on the CEST measure were not related to any of the responsibility questions (all rs < .10, ps > .07). Participants' response to the Linda problem was positively related to responsibility assigned to state law (r = .14, p < .05), and the victim (r = .16, p < .01), indicating that the more experientially participants were processing, the more they assigned responsibility to state law and the victim.

Correlational analyses were conducted among all of the responsibility questions (see Table 5). Results revealed that responsibility assigned to Biblical authority was related to responsibility assigned to two other entities. The more responsibility assigned to "Biblical authority," the more assigned to "victim" (r = .229, p < .001), and the more responsibility assigned to "chance" (r = .164, p < .01).

Assigning responsibility to "chance" was also positively related to assigning responsibility to the "defendant" (r = .144, p < .01) and the "victim" (r = .329, p < .001) and was negatively related to "judge's instructions/state law" (r = -.122, p < .05).
*Additionally, "judge's instructions/state law" responsibility was positively correlated with "juror"* responsibility (r = .169, p < .01). Ratings for "Victim" were positively related to "Defendant" (r = -.121, p < .05).

## Dependent Variable Four: General Feelings of Retribution and Mercy

A 3-way MANOVA was performed with answers to four questions regarding retribution and mercy in general (e.g., "Criminals should be shown mercy" and "Murderers deserve the death penalty because they killed") as dependent variables.

## Effects of Case Type

As in study one, no predictions were made for case type (high aggravators or high mitigators), and analysis revealed that this variable did not affect feelings of retribution and mercy (F (4,303) = .60, p > .05).

Table 5: Correlations among responsibility questions

| | Judge's instructions | Biblical authority | Juror | Defendant | Chance | Victim |
|---|---|---|---|---|---|---|
| Judge's instruc-tions/ state law | - | -.176** | 0.068 | 0.034 | .334** | -.221** |
| Biblical authority | -0.043 | - | 0.062 | 0.092 | -.331** | .767** |
| Juror | .169** | 0.062 | - | .371** | 0.022 | 0.069 |
| Defendant | 0.12 | 0.092 | .371** | - | 0.104 | 0.064 |
| Chance | -.122* | -.331** | 0.022 | 0.104 | - | -.371** |
| Victim | 0.022 | .767** | 0.069 | 0.064 | -.371** | - |

- p < .05
- ** p < .0

## Effects of Appeals

It was expected that the religious appeal group would be the most supportive of general notions of retribution and the least supportive of forgiveness than no-appeal group or the non-religious appeal group, which would be the least supportive of retribution and the most supportive of forgiveness. Analyses did not support these hypotheses (F $(8,608) = 1.09$, p $> .05$).

## Effects of Directives

Analyses indicated that directives did not influence answers to these statements (F $(8,608) = .79$, p $> .05$).

## Interactions

No interactions were predicted among case type, appeal, and directive, and none were found (Fs $< 1.46$, ps $> .17$).

## Correlations among Feelings of Retribution/Mercy Questions and CEST Processing

Correlational analyses reveal that answers to the Linda problem were not related to the participant's feelings about forgiveness and retribution (all rs $< .10$, ps $> .08$). On the other hand, there was a relationship between CEST scores and three of these variables. The higher the score on the CEST scale (indicating more experiential thinking), the less agreement that criminals should be forgiven (r $= -.161$, p $< .01$), and more agreement that the criminal deserves death (r $= .250$, p $< .001$) and "payback" for their crimes (r $= .145$, p $< .05$).

Dependent Variable Five: Factors that Influenced Decisions

It was also of interest to determine what factors (e.g., judge's instructions, Biblical authority, prosecutor's arguments) influenced participants' decisions. Although no specific hypotheses were made, an exploratory analysis was conducted. A 3-way MANOVA was performed with these twelve factors as dependent variables.

<u>Effects of Appeals</u>

The type of appeal significantly affected answers to the questions regarding what influenced their decision (F (24,586) = 1.92, p < .05). Univariate analyses showed that this effect was due to the influence of "Biblical authority," "prosecution arguments," "personal religious beliefs," and "personal feelings about the death penalty."

Being influenced by "Biblical authority" was significantly affected by appeal type (F (2,303) = 11.71, p < .001). The religious appeal group (M = 3.67) was significantly more influenced by the Bible than the non-religious appeal group (M = 2.78; p < .01), and the no-appeal group (M = 2.49; p < .001). The non-religious appeal and no-appeal groups were not significantly different (p > .05).

Similarly, the influence of "prosecution arguments" was significantly affected by appeal type (F (2,303) = 3.64, p < .05). The religious group (M = 4.26) was not significantly different from the non-religious group (M = 3.97; p > .05) or the no-appeal group (M = 4.52; p > .05), but the no-appeal group was significantly more influenced by the prosecutor's arguments than the non-religious appeal group (p < .01).

The influence of "personal religious beliefs" was also affected by appeal type (F (2,303) = 5.58, p < .01). The religious group (M = 3.46) was not significantly different from the non-religious group (M = 2.90; p > .05), but was significantly more influenced by personal religious beliefs than the no-appeal group (M = 2.62; p > .01). The non-religious and no-appeal groups were not significantly different from one another (p > .05).

Finally, appeal type affected the influence of "personal feelings about the death penalty" (F (2,303) = 3.17, p < .05). The religious group (M = 4.34) was not significantly different from the non-religious group (M = 4.11; p > .05), but was significantly more influenced by personal feelings than the no-appeal group (M = 3.74; p < .05). The non-religious and no-appeal groups were not significantly different from one another (p > .05).

In sum, the religious appeal group was generally more influenced by Biblical authority and personal religious beliefs, while the no-appeal group was more influenced by the prosecution arguments and the non-religious group was more influenced by personal feelings about the death penalty. This finding suggests that appeals are exerting some effect on participants' decision-making, even if the effects do not translate into differences in verdict confidence scores.

## Effects of Directives

Directives did not affect the answers to the questions about factors that influenced decisions (F (24,586) = 1.2, p > .05).

## Effects of Case Type

Case type had a significant effect on answers to the influence items (F (12,292) = 2.06, p < .05). This effect was a result of the measure "prosecutor's arguments" (F (1, 303) = 9.50, p < .05). Participants in the high aggravator case (M = 4.45) were more influenced by the prosecutor's arguments than participants in the high mitigator case (M = 4.08). This finding was also found in Study One.

The influence of "defense attorney arguments" was also affected by case type (F (1, 303) = 16.3, p < .01). Participants in the high aggravator case (M = 4.2) were less influenced by the defense attorney's arguments than participants in the high mitigator case (M = 4.64). In sum, when the case type was high in aggravators, the prosecutor was more influential; and when the case type was high in mitigators, the defense attorney was more influential.

Interactions

No interactions were predicted among case type, appeal, and directive, and none were found (Fs < 1.29, ps > .09.)

Correlations among "Influence" questions and CEST processing

Correlational analyses revealed correlations between answers on the Linda problem and several of the "influence" questions.    First, there was a positive relationship between the Linda problem (high scores mean more experiential thinking) and being influenced by "feelings about the death penalty (r = .16, p < .01), "my feelings about the case" (r = .13, p < .05), and "my instincts about the case" (r = .12, p < .05), indicating that the more experientially participants processed information, the more they were influenced by their feelings about the death penalty, their feelings about the case and their instincts about the case.  CEST scores did not correlate with any of the items on the "influence" list (rs < .07, ps > .20).

Correlational analyses were performed among the 12 "influence" questions and revealed numerous significant correlations. Thus, only thee correlations involving Biblical authority are reported here.  Replicating findings from Study One, Biblical authority was negatively correlated with judicial instructions, (r = -.15, p < .01), and positively correlated with personal religious beliefs (r = .78, p < .001). Being influenced by Biblical authority was also related to being influenced by feelings about the death penalty (r = .37, p < .001),[5] instincts about the case (r = .16, p < .01), and feelings about the defendant (r = .16, p < .01).[6] As opposed to Study One, Biblical authority was not related to evidence (r = -.06, p > .05).

---

[5] This correlation was not significant in Study One
[6] The "instincts about the case" and "feelings about the defendant" questions were not asked in Study One.

## Individual Differences

Individual difference measures were analyzed to measure their relationship to the dependent measures. These individual differences include gender, age, fundamentalism, evangelism, devotionalism, literal interpretism, and the REI measure.[7]

## Gender

Since gender is often an important variable in decision-making and exerted a main effect in Study 1, all principal analyses were repeated, using gender as a fourth independent variable. Only results that were altered by the addition of gender will be reported below.

**Verdict confidence.** Analyses revealed that, contrary to the findings from Study One, there was not a main effect for gender ($F_{(1,282)} = .02$, $p > .05$). Similarly, there were no changes in main effects for appeals, case type, or directive, nor were there any changes in the results regarding the interactions. There was, an unexpected four-way interaction ($F_{(4,282)} = 3.30$, $p < .05$); however this interaction was uninterpretable and many groups had a very small number of participants.

**CEST measures.** There was not a main effect for gender on the CEST measure ($F_{(1,275)} = .69$, $p > .05$) or the Linda problem ($F_{(1,314)} = 3.70$, $p > .05$). Adding gender did not change the results regarding the main effects of directives, appeals or case type on the CEST scale or the Linda problem. Nor did adding gender affect the interaction found between case type and directive on the Linda problem or the interaction results on the CEST measure.

---

[7] Religious affiliation was also included as an independent measure, however these analyses did not contribute any significant findings. Thus these analyses will not be reported.

<u>Perception of responsibility</u>. There was a main effect of gender on the responsibility questions (F (6,281) = 3.84, p < .01). Gender significantly affected answers to three questions. First, males (M= 4.97) were less likely than females (M = 5.55) to find "judge's instructions/state law" responsible for their sentencing decision (F (1,286) = 8.49, p < .01). Second, males (M = 2.43) were also less likely than females (M = 2.68) to find "chance" responsible (F (1,286) = 3.97, p < .05). Finally, males (M = 3.74) were less likely than females (M = 4.29) to find the "victim" responsible (F (1,286) = 10.23, p < .01).

The results regarding the main effects of case type, appeal and directive, and interactions found in the three-way did not change when gender was added to the model.

<u>General feelings of retribution and mercy</u>. Gender did not have an effect on feelings of retribution and mercy (F (4,282) = 1.56, p > .05). The results regarding the main effects and interactions found in the three-way did not change when gender was added to the model.

<u>Factors that influenced decisions</u>. Gender did have an effect on ratings of factors that influenced decisions (F (12,272) = 3.06, p < .001). Univariate analysis indicate that males were less likely than females to be influenced by "prosecution arguments" (M = 4.08 vs. 4.38; F (1,283) = 4.88, p < .05), "feelings about the case" (M = 4.04 vs. 4.38; F (1,283) = 10.79, p < .01), and "instincts about the case" (M = 4.11 vs. 4.83; F (1,283) = 10.54, p < .01).

Although adding gender did not affect results regarding directive or the interactions among the dependent variables, the results regarding the effects of appeals were slightly different. Just like in the three-way analysis, the type of appeal significantly affected answers to the questions regarding what influenced their decision, and univariate analyses showed that this effect was due to the influence of "Biblical authority," "prosecution arguments," "personal religious beliefs," and "personal feelings about the death penalty." However, in the four-way, the effect was also due to defense attorney arguments (F (1,283) = 3.24, p <

.05). The religious group (M = 4.36) was not significantly different from the non-religious group (M = 4.23; p > .05), or from the no-appeal group (M = 4.70; p > .05), but the no-appeal group was significantly more influenced by defense attorney arguments than the non-religious group (p < .05).

Finally, the addition of gender to the model changed the results regarding case type. In the three -way, case type affected the answers to the "influence" questions, however when gender was added, case type no longer influenced the answers (F (12,272) = 1.38, p > .05).

In sum, analyses revealed that there was not an effect for gender on verdict confidence, the CEST measure, or feelings of retribution or mercy. There was an effect of gender on the responsibility questions, with females being more likely than males to place responsibility on "judge's instructions/state law," "chance," and the "victim." Further, females were more likely than males to be influenced by "prosecution arguments," "feelings about the case," and "instincts about the case."

<u>Age</u>

Pearson's correlation indicated that age was not related to verdict confidence (r = .102, p > .05).

<u>Fundamentalism</u>

Individuals who scored high on the fundamentalism scale were expected to be more likely to vote for the death penalty than those scoring low on the fundamentalism scale. Analyses indicated that there was no correlation between fundamentalism and verdict confidence (r = -.04, p > .05).

## Evangelism

It was expected that evangelical individuals would be less likely to vote for the death penalty than those individuals who were not evangelical. A Pearson's correlation conducted between scores on the evangelism scale and verdict confidence was not significant ($r = .04$, $p > .05$).

A second measure of evangelism (a "yes" or "no" answer to the question "Have you ever tried to encourage someone to believe in Jesus Christ or to accept Jesus Christ as his or her savior?") also did not affect verdict confidence ($t (318) = .15$, $p > .05$).

## Devotionalism

Counter to the hypothesis, the devotionalism scale was not correlated with verdict confidence ($r = .06$, $p > .05$). An interaction between case type and the devotionalism scale was predicted; it was expected that the greater amount of time a participant spent engaged in religious activities, the more influential religious appeals would be on the participant's decision-making. Participants were grouped as "low" or "high" in devotionalism based on the median split. A four-way ANOVA was performed, with devotionalism, appeal, directive and case type as independent variables, and verdict confidence as the dependent variable. There was a marginal main effect for devotionalism ($F (1,282) = 3.55$, $p < .06$). As predicted, those who were low in devotionalism ($M = 2.33$) were more in favor of the death penalty than those high in devotionalism ($M = 3.65$). However there was no main effect for appeal ($F (2,282) = .54$, $p > .05$), nor were there any interactions among the variables ($Fs < 1.78$, $ps > .17$).

The single devotionalism item was not correlated with verdict confidence ($r = .035$, $p > .05$).

## Literal Interpretism

It was predicted that, in the no-appeal condition, those who felt the Bible should be interpreted literally (i.e., a "yes" answer to the question "Do you believe that the Bible is the actual word of God and is to be taken literally, word for word?") would be more likely to support the death penalty than those individuals who did not believe in a strict translation. However, in the religious appeal condition, the effect was expected to be reversed because participants were exposed to a religious mercy appeal. Thus, in the religious appeal condition, participants who were literal interpreters would believe that the mercy messages were the actual word of God, and be less supportive of a death sentence.

Literal interpretism was added to the main model as a fourth independent variable and an ANOVA was conducted with verdict confidence as a dependent variable. Contrary to the hypothesis, literal interpreters scored lower on the verdict confidence measure ($M = 2.11$) and thus were more likely to sentence the defendant to death, than participants who were not literal interpreters ($M = 3.50$, $F (1,278) = 7.46$, $p < .01$). Furthermore, there was no interaction between literal interpretism and appeal ($F (2,278) = .71$, $p > .05$). Thus, all literal interpreters were more likely than non-literal interpreters to sentence the defendant to death, even those who received the religious mercy appeal.

## CEST Processing Style

As in Study 1, It was hypothesized that individuals scoring high on the NFC sub-scale of the REI would be more "rational" on the CEST measures and individuals scoring high on the FI sub-scale would be more "experiential" on the CEST measures. Analyses revealed that scores on the CEST scale were related to scores on the NFC scale ($r = -.18$, $p < .05$), indicating that the more rational a person was on the NFC scale, the more rational his/her scores on the CEST scale. On the other hand, scores on the CEST measure were not related to scores on the FI scale ($r = -.06$, $p > .05$).

The Linda problem was related to scores on the FI scale (r = .12, p < .05), suggesting that individuals who processed more experientially on the Linda problem also scored more experientially on the CEST measure. Scores on the Linda problem were not related to scores on the NFC scale (r = -.05, p > .05). Further, the NFC and FI scores were not correlated (r = .04, p > .05).

<u>Verdict confidence</u>. Participants were separated into either a "high NFC" or "low NFC" group and either a "low FI" or "high FI" group according to median splits. A five-way ANOVA was conducted with case type, appeal, directive, NFC, and FI as independent variables and verdict confidence as a dependent variable. There were no main effects for case type, appeals, directives, or NFC (Fs < .95, ps > .39). There was a main effect for FI (F (1,248) = 4.61, p < .05) that indicated that low FI individuals (M = 3.11) were more in favor of life than high FI individuals (M = 2.8).

Contrary to the hypotheses, there was no interaction between case type and NFC (F (1,248) = 1.1, p > .05), nor was there an interaction between case type and FI (F (1,248) = .15, p > .05), indicating that FI and NFC did not affect weighting of aggravating and mitigating circumstances.

There was an interaction between appeal and case type (F (1,248) = 3.44, p < .05). When individuals received a religious appeal (t (90) = 2.9, p <.01), or a non-religious appeal (t (112) = 3.24, p <.01), they were able to weigh aggravators and mitigators properly (i.e., the means for the high mitigators case type were significantly more in favor of life than the high aggravators case type), whereas when participants did not receive an appeal (t (113) = 1.65, p > .05), they were not able to weigh aggravators and mitigators properly.

There were four-way interactions: between case type, appeal, directive and NFC (F (1,248) = 2.67, p < .05), between case type, appeal, FI and NFC (F (1,248) = 8.87, p < .05), between case type, directive, FI and NFC (F (1,248)

= 3.24, p < .05) and between directive, appeal, NFC, and FI (F (1,248) = 3.7, p < .05). All of these interactions were uninterpretable and many groups had very small numbers of participants.

<u>Relationship between REI and responsibility questions</u>. Correlational analyses were performed among the NFC and FI scales and the questions regarding which entities the participant felt were responsible for the sentencing decision. Scores on the NFC scale were positively related to finding the "judge's instructions/state law" responsible (r = .19, p < .01), and finding the "defendant responsible" (r = .14, p < .01), indicating that the more rational the participant's score on the NFC scale, the more responsibility the participant placed on these entities. NFC scores were negatively related to finding the "victim responsible" (r = -.17, p < .01), finding "Biblical authority" responsible (r = -.17, p < .01) and finding "chance" responsible (r = -.25, p < .001), signifying that the more rational the individual, the less responsibility placed on these entities. Scores on the NFC scale did not correlate with finding "juror" responsible (r = .10, p > .05). Scores on the FI scale did not correlate with any of the responsibility measures (all rs< .09, ps > .19).

<u>Relationship between REI and attitudes about mercy and payback</u>. Correlational analyses between the NFC score and the questions regarding mercy and retribution revealed a negative relationship between NFC and "criminals deserve payback" (r = -.13, p < .05), suggesting that the more rational the NFC score, the less agreement with this sentence. Correlations with other questions regarding mercy and retribution were not significant (all rs < .11, ps > .05). The only question that correlated with FI scores was "Murderers deserve death" (r = .15, p < .01), indicating that the more experiential participants were on the FI scale, the more they agreed with this statement. This finding is in line with the main effect on verdict confidence, which indicated

that more experiential thinkers were more in favor of the death sentence. The other questions were not significantly related to the FI scale (all rs< .10, ps > .05).

Relationship between REI and factors that are influential. Additional analyses were conducted to investigate relationships between the REI scales and the questions regarding factors that were influential to the participant's sentencing decision. FI scores were positively related to being influenced by "feelings about the case" (r = .14, p < .05), "instincts about the case" (r = .24, p < .01), and "feelings about the defendant" (r = .14, p < .05), indicating that the more experientially persons scored on the FI scale, the more they relied on these factors.

Analyses revealed that the more rational a participant's NFC score, the more s/he relied on "judges instructions" (r = .32, p < .001), "evidence" (r = .18, p < .01), and "logic and reason" (r = .13, p < .05), and the less s/he relied on "Biblical authority" (r = -.13, p < .05), "instincts" (r = .11, p < .05), and "feelings about the defendant" (r = .22, p < .001). No other questions on the NFC scale or the FI scale correlated with any influence measures (all rs < .1, ps > .05).

Summary of Individual Difference Measures

Verdict confidence was not associated with gender, age, fundamentalism, evangelism, or NFC scores. However, high experiential thinkers (high FI scores) were more in favor of a death sentence than low experiential thinkers. Devotionalism had a marginal effect on verdict confidence: Those who were low in devotionalism were more in favor of the death penalty than those high in devotionalism. Literal interpreters were more likely to sentence the defendant to death, even in the religious appeal condition, where the participant read Biblical appeals for mercy. Finally, case type did not interact with devotionalism, FI or NFC, indicating that these factors do not affect the ability to weigh aggravators and mitigators.

Analyses revealed that gender did not affect scores on the CEST scale or the Linda problem. Scores on the CEST scale were negatively related to the NFC scale, indicating that rational processing on the CEST scale was associated with rational processing on the NFC scale. Similarly, scores on the Linda problem were positively related to the FI scale, indicating that experiential processing on the Linda problem was associated with experiential processing on the FI scale.

There was an effect of gender on the responsibility questions, with females being more likely than males to place responsibility on judge's instructions/state law, chance, and the victim. While FI scores were not related to the perceived responsibility questions, high NFC scores were associated with placing more responsibility on judge's instructions/state law and the defendant, and less responsibility on the victim, Biblical authority and chance.

There was no relationship between feelings of mercy and retribution and gender, but there was a negative relationship between NFC scores and agreement with the "criminals deserve payback" question, and a positive relationship between FI scores with and agreement with the "murderers deserve death" question.

There was a gender effect on the influence questions: Females were more likely than males to be influenced by prosecution arguments, feelings about the case, and instincts about the case. In addition, FI scores were positively related to being influenced by feelings about the case, feelings about the defendant, and instincts about the case. NFC scores were positively related to judge's instructions/state law, evidence, logic and reason, and negatively related to Biblical authority, instincts, and feelings about the defendant.

## DISCUSSION

### CEST Processing

Contrary to the hypotheses, directives did not affect CEST processing on either the Linda problem or the CEST scale. This suggests that the directive may not have been strong enough to alter participants' processing, or that the directive may have occurred too long before the CEST measures to be effective. Similarly, appeals did not affect CEST processing on either the Linda problem or the CEST scale. This result was also produced in Study One and represents further evidence that appeals do not affect rational or experiential processing.

An unexpected effect was found for case type on the CEST measure: Participants in the high aggravators condition were more experiential than those in the high mitigators condition. An interaction between directives and case type on the Linda problem suggested that the no-directive participants also processed more experientially if they read the high aggravators case than if they read the high mitigators case. It is possible that the emotion produced by reading the high aggravator case was enough to lead to experiential processing, although it is unclear why this would only occur only in the control condition when measured with the Linda problem.

### Verdict Confidence

Analyses revealed that the case type manipulation was successful. Participants reading the case facts containing high aggravators were more likely to sentence the defendant to death than participants reading the case facts containing high mitigators.

Neither appeals nor directives affected verdict confidence scores. Additionally, none of the expected interactions were found, indicating that appeals and directives did not affect the ability to weigh aggravators and mitigators properly. As these finding replicate those in Study One, it is likely that these factors do not affect jurors' sentencing decisions. Although more realistic tests may reveal an effect of appeals, initial indications are that religious appeals do not limit jurors' ability to make decisions.

Although Study One found a significant positive correlation between scores on the CEST scale and verdict confidence, this effect was not replicated in Study Two. Thus, further research is required to determine whether processing type is related to sentencing decisions.

Perceptions of Responsibility

Perceptions of responsibility were not affected by case type, appeals, directives or interactions among these variables. These items were also not affected by scores on the CEST scale, however there was a positive relationship between the Linda problem and responsibility assigned to state law and to the victim, indicating that the more experientially  participants were processing, the more they assigned responsibility to these entities.

Correlations performed among these responsibility factors revealed that the more responsibility an individual assigned to Biblical authority, the more they assigned to the victim and to chance. The correlation between responsibility assigned to Biblical authority and responsibility assigned to the jurors that was found in Study One was not replicated here, casting doubt on the notion that Biblical authority poses a threat to the legal system because it decreases jurors' perceptions of personal responsibility.

General Feelings of Retribution and Mercy

Feelings of retribution and mercy were not affected by case type, appeals, directives or interactions among these variables. These items also were not affected by scores on the Linda problem, however there were relationships between scores on the CEST scale and the retribution and mercy questions. Taken together, the findings from these three items indicated that experiential processing was associated with more positive feelings toward retribution and more negative feelings toward mercy. These findings replicated those in Study One.

Factors that Influenced Decisions

Although directives did not affect answers to the questions regarding factors that influenced participants' decision, appeals significantly affected answers to these questions. The religious appeal group was generally more influenced by Biblical authority and personal religious beliefs, while the no-appeal group was more influenced by the prosecution arguments and the non-religious group was more influenced by personal feelings about the death penalty. It is interesting that the religious group admitted to being influenced by the Bible more, although appeals did not lead to differences in verdicts. It is possible that religious appeals increased the salience of Biblical authority, leading participants to rely on it more. Participants may also have felt that it was more acceptable to admit their reliance on Biblical authority since the attorney told them to do so.

Case type also affected responses to the influence questions. The high aggravators case facts led to more reported reliance on the prosecutor's arguments, while the high mitigators case facts led to greater reliance on the defense attorney's arguments. These results, along with those from Study One, support the idea that participants are more influenced by the arguments that are more in line with their feelings about the sentence that the defendant should receive.

While CEST scores were not related to answers on the influence questions, experiential processing on the Linda problem was related to being influenced by feelings about the death penalty, feelings about the case, and instincts about the case. These results indicated that the Linda problem is accurately measuring experiential processing, as it is related to relying on more emotional, as opposed to rational, factors.

Correlational analyses among the influence questions were numerous, however the most relevant correlations were the ones that involved Biblical authority. The more participants relied on Biblical authority, the more they relied on personal religious beliefs, feelings about the death penalty, their instincts and their feelings about the defendant. These results suggest that the influence of Biblical authority is related to several experiential and emotionally driven factors and needs to be explored further.

Individual differences

Verdict confidence scores were not related to gender, age, fundamentalism, evangelism, FI scores or NFC scores. Further, case type did not interact with devotionalism, FI or NFC, indicating that these factors did not affect the ability to weigh aggravators and mitigators. This suggests that these factors do not threaten proper legal decision-making in this way.

<u>Religious scales</u>

Those who were low in devotionalism were more in favor of the death penalty than those high in devotionalism, supporting previous research (Young, 1992). An interaction between literal interpretism and appeals was expected in that participants in the control and no-appeal conditions would be more in favor of the death penalty than participants in the religious appeal condition, since the latter group heard Biblical mercy appeals. This interaction was not significant, although there was a main effect for literal interpretism. Literal interpreters were more likely to sentence the defendant to death, even in the religious appeal condition, where the participant read Biblical appeals for mercy. This replicates the findings of Study One and supports the findings of Young (1992). Such findings have implications for the legal system. For example, an attorney in a capital punishment case could base jury selection decisions on factors such as devotionalsim and literal interpretism.

## Gender

Analyses revealed that there was not an effect for gender on the CEST measures or feelings of retribution or mercy items. There was an effect of gender on the responsibility questions, with females being more likely than males to place responsibility on "judge's instructions/state law," "chance," and the "victim." Further, females were more likely than males to be influenced by "prosecution arguments," "feelings about the case," and "instincts about the case." The effects of gender on verdict confidence found in Study One were not replicated in Study Two, casting doubt on the ability of gender to influence sentencing decisions. Thus, Study Two adds little to the knowledge of gender effects on juror decision-making in capital trials.

## Rational-Experiential Inventory (REI)

Rational processing on the CEST scale was associated with rational processing on the NFC scale. Similarly, experiential processing on the Linda problem was associated with experiential processing on the FI scale. These effects were not found in Study One, so they should be interpreted with caution; however, it is encouraging that these measures were related to the processing types they were meant to measure.

High NFC scores were associated with placing more responsibility on judge's instructions/state law and the defendant, and less responsibility on the victim, Biblical authority and chance. Additionally, NFC scores were positively related to being influenced by judge's instructions/state law, evidence, logic and reason, and negatively related to reliance on Biblical authority, instincts, and feelings about the defendant. These results generally support the findings of Study One and suggest that behaviors of participants high in NFC comport with "rational" juror behavior.

Conversely, FI scores were positively related to being influenced by feelings about the case, feelings about the defendant, and instincts about the case. This suggests that jurors high in FI tend to be influenced more by emotional or experiential factors than "rational" factors that jurors are supposed to rely on (e.g., the evidence).

In sum, Study Two provided further support for the finding in Study One that emotional appeals do not affect jury decision-making. Although religious variables (e.g., being influenced by Biblical authority) did provide some interesting information about how religion affects decision-making, verdict confidence scores were not affected by the manipulation of religious appeals. In addition, Study Two found that neither retributive appeals nor directives affected processing type. Further research is needed to determine whether these findings are truly indicative of the relationships between the variables, or whether the manipulations used in these studies simply failed to capture these effects.

# CHAPTER 11

# Discussion, Limitations and Future Studies

## GENERAL DISCUSSION

The use of religious appeals in closing arguments is a controversial issue that has prompted judicial responses ranging from total prohibition to total acceptance of such appeals. Although court holdings have varied greatly, all have been based on assumptions about the influence (or lack of influence) religious appeals have on juror decision-making. This research addressed these assumptions by applying a dual processing model of decision-making called Cognitive-Experiential Self-Theory (CEST; Epstein, 1990).

This research addressed six specific questions regarding appeals and their effect on mock jurors' decision-making. Results related to each of these research questions have implications for court decisions regarding the use of religious appeals in closing arguments.

### Do Appeals Affect Jurors' Ability to Weigh Aggravators and Mitigators?

The first research question asked whether appeals affect jurors' ability to weigh aggravators and mitigators properly. Overall, participants were successful at weighing aggravators and migtigators, regardless of whether or not they received an appeal. Thus, both studies found that religious appeals did not negatively affect participants' ability to weigh aggravators and mitigators properly.

Similarly, appeals did not affect verdicts in either study. Though religious appeals did not affect the number of death sentences, appeals did affect reports of the factors that influenced participants' decisions. In Study Two, the religious appeal group reported being more influenced by Biblical authority and personal religious beliefs than the non-religious appeal or no-appeal groups. The religious appeal may have made religion more salient to participants who otherwise would not have thought about what religious authority has to say about the death penalty. It is also possible that participants in the religious appeal condition were more willing to admit being influenced by Biblical authority because the use of the appeal by the attorney led participants to believe that relying on Biblical authority was acceptable. Because this effect was found only in Study Two, these results should be interpreted with caution.

Although religious appeals did not affect verdicts, it is interesting that overall verdict confidence scores from Study 1 (which used a retributive appeal; M = 1.81) were significantly lower (i.e., more in favor of death) than verdict confidence scores from Study Two (which used mercy appeals M = 3.18; t (714) 3.14 p < .01) Because the trial summaries in Study One and Study Two were identical except for the type of appeal (retribution or mercy), this difference could be due to the appeals used. Since there are other factors that could account for this difference, this explanation is merely speculative.

While religious appeals did not affect actual sentencing decisions, there was evidence that religion was associated with factors that influence decisions. For example, reliance on Biblical authority was negatively associated with reliance on judge's instructions/state law (both studies), and reliance on the evidence (Study One). Additionally, reliance on Biblical authority was correlated with reliance on personal religious beliefs (both studies). These relationships indicate that individuals who rely on religious authority may make jury decisions in improper ways (e.g., by not relying on the law or evidence).

## Do Both Prosecutorial and Defense Appeals Affect Decision-making?

A related research question involves whether both prosecutorial and defense appeals affect decision-making. These two studies indicate that neither prosecutorial nor defense appeals affect verdicts or the ability to weigh aggravators and mitigators. These findings support the notion that religious appeals do not affect juror decision-making in legally impermissible ways.

In sum, the results of these initial studies indicate that fears about religious appeals affecting the proper weighing of aggravators and mitigators may be unfounded. Appeals did not affect verdicts or participants' abilities to weigh aggravators and mitigators, but they were positively related to reported reliance on extra-legal sources (e.g., personal religious beliefs) and negatively related to reliance on legal authority and evidence.

## Does Cognitive-Experiential Self-Theory Explain Differences in Decision-making?

The overall findings regarding Cognitive-Experiential Self-Theory (CEST) call the theory's validity into question. Neither appeals nor directives affected processing on the CEST measures (i.e., the Linda problem and the CEST scale). It is possible that the manipulations used were not strong enough to trigger experiential processing. In a real trial, appeals may be more likely to affect jurors' emotions (and thus trigger experiential processing) than in the written trial summaries used in these studies. Alternatively, Biblical authority may have triggered some level of experiential processing, just not enough to show up on CEST measures. Biblical authority was related to experiential influences (e.g., relying on instincts or blaming the victim; Study Two) and negatively related to some more rational influences (e.g., placing responsibility on jurors; Study One). Thus, it is possible that Biblical authority did affect processing style, though the effects were not strong enough to show up on CEST measures.

Directives may not have been successful at influencing CEST processing style because the directives used in this study were quite different than those used in previous studies (Epstein, 1992, 1996). Previous studies gave directives that clearly instructed the participant to process information in a certain manner (rationally or experientially) while completing the CEST measure. Here, they were given instructions about how to make the sentencing decision (rationally or experientially), and then later completed the CEST measure without being given the directive again. Thus, a directive concerning how to process while making a sentencing decision may not carry over to the CEST measure. Additionally, there was a sizable time delay (usually about 30 minutes) between the directive and the CEST measure, so any effect of the directive could have worn off. If these explanations are correct, they suggest that the generalizabilty of the CEST theory is severely limited.

The appeal and directive manipulations may have been unable to affect processing type due to a ceiling effect. In Study One, only 38 participants (15%) were processing rationally as measured by the Linda problem and 84 (33%) were processing rationally on the CEST measure. In Study Two, only 37 (11%) were processing rationally on the Linda problem and 95 (29%) were processing rationally on the CEST measure.

This ceiling effect could indicate that most people typically process in an experiential manner. A second possible explanation is that reading about a murder could have caused enough emotion to trigger experiential processing in most participants. This explanation is partially supported by the main effect of case type in Study Two. Participants who read the high aggravators case type (with a more graphic and potentially more emotion-provoking crime), processed more experientially on the

CEST measure than participants who read the high mitigators case type. The interaction between case type and directive on the Linda problem indicated the same pattern; there was more experiential processing in the high aggravators case, although only in the no-directive condition. As this pattern was found only in Study Two, the conclusions that can be made are somewhat limited.

The failure to find the expected results regarding CEST processing could also be a result of a failure of the CEST measures. The Linda problem did not even correlate with the CEST scale in Study One, even though both measures were intended to measure processing style. Neither the CEST scale nor the Linda Problem were related to the REI individual difference processing measures (FI and NFC) in Study One. Study Two results were more promising; the two measures were correlated with each other and also with the FI and NFC scales. Specifically, the FI scale correlated with the Linda problem, indicating that the more experiential the FI score, the more experiential the score on the Linda problem. Similarly, scores on the NFC scale correlated with the CEST scale, suggesting that rational scores on NFC were related to rational CEST scores. While significant, these correlations were fairly low, suggesting that they should be treated with some caution.

On the other hand, the CEST scale and Linda problem were related to other measures in ways that suggest that they were properly measuring processing style. For example, experiential thinkers (as measured by the CEST scale) relied less on the judge's instructions/state law (Study One). Hypothetically, experiential thinkers would rely more on emotion than on more "rational" factors such as the instructions or law. Similarly, several Study Two findings indicate a link between experiential thinking on the Linda problem and "experiential type" juror behavior, such as being influence by feelings or blaming the victim. Experiential scores were positively correlated with being influenced by feelings about the death penalty, feelings about the case, and instincts about the case (Study Two).

Experiential processors were also more likely to place responsibility on the victim (Study Two). Since these items are experiential in nature (as opposed to more rational items such as being influenced by the evidence or law), these correlations support the notion that the Linda problem was accurately measuring experiential processing. As these results were not consistent across studies, they should be considered with caution. In sum, the CEST measures produced mixed findings, casting some doubt on their ability to accurately measure processing style and questioning the validity of the CEST theory.

## Do Appeals Reduce Responsibility for the Sentencing Decision?

Appeals did not affect the amount of responsibility participants placed on themselves as jurors. However correlations performed among the responsibility factors revealed that Biblical authority was related to undesirable influences. For example, the more responsibility an individual assigned to Biblical authority, the more s/he assigned to the victim (Study Two) and to chance (both studies), and the less s/he assigned to jurors (Study One). In addition, the more a participant reported being influenced by Biblical authority, the more s/he was influenced by personal religious beliefs, feelings about the death penalty, instincts, and feelings about the defendant.[8] The courts that were concerned that religious appeals would affect personal responsibility for the sentencing decision (*People v. Wash*, 1993; *Sandoval v. Calderon*, 2000) would likely be concerned that these relationships with Biblical authority exist, especially the finding that participants who placed high responsibility on Biblical authority placed less responsibility on themselves as jurors.

Because religious appeals did not affect the amount of personal responsibility jurors placed on themselves, fears

---

[8] Both studies found the correlation between Biblical authority and personal religious beliefs, however the other variables were used only in Study Two

about religious appeals affecting perceptions of personal responsibility may be unfounded. More research is needed to fully investigate the relationships between Biblical authority and responsibility placed on the jurors and other entities.

Do Different Types of Directives Affect Jury Decision-making?

The next research question involved the directives that instructed participants in how to make their decisions (experientially or rationally). As with religious appeals, directives did not affect the ability of participants to weigh aggravators and mitigators in either study. Manipulation checks in Study Two suggest that the manipulations were not strong; many participants were not sensitive to the appeals. Directives did affect the factors that influenced participants' decisions, however. For example, in Study One, participants who received a rational directive relied more on the evidence, and participants receiving an experiential instruction relied more on their personal religious beliefs. Because these findings were not replicated in Study Two, further research is needed to discover the limits of these relationships.

Do Individual Differences Affect Jury Decision-making?

Gender affected verdict confidence scores in Study One, indicating that men were more likely to sentence the defendant to death than women. This finding supports those found in previous studies (Sandys & McGarrell, 1995; Whitehead & Blankenship, 2000), however Study Two did not replicate this finding. Although the Study Two means suggest that men were more likely than women to give a death sentence, the difference was not statistically significant.

Two of the religious attitude scales produced differences in sentencing: Devotionalism and literal interpretism. The other religious scales (fundamentalism and evangelism) did not affect sentencing in either study. Individuals who were low in devotionalism were more likely to sentence the defendant to death than those high in devotionalism, although this result was found only in Study Two.

It is not surprising that a belief in a literal interpretation of the Bible was associated with an increase in death sentences in Study One, when participants were given a retributive Biblical appeal (e.g. "an eye for an eye"). It is interesting, though that this same effect was found in Study Two, when participants were presented with a Biblical appeal for mercy (e.g., "turn the other cheek"). Why literal interpreters did not treat the mercy appeal as a literal instruction is uncertain.

The findings for devotionalism and literal interpretism could have important implications for voir dire, as attorneys could make jury selection based on potential jurors' answers to questions designed to target these factors. A recent decision handed down by the Third Circuit (*U.S. v. DeJesus*, 2003) addressed the permissibility of striking potential jurors based on religion. The court held that, while eliminating jurors on the basis of a particular religion is prohibited, it is acceptable to eliminate jurors on the basis of how often they practice religion. Thus, it would be permitted to remove potential jurors based on their devotionalism and beliefs regarding literal interterpretism.

Previous studies investigating the relationship between NFC and verdicts have produced a variety of results. One study found that mock jurors who scored high on the NFC scale were more defense-oriented (DeWitt, Richardson & Warner, 1997), another found that high-NFC participants were more likely to view a criminal who made a questionable confession as guilty (Graziano, Panter & Tanaka, 1990), and two others found no relationship between NFC and verdicts (Bornstein, 2004; Lester, Slaw Briggs, & Scanlan, 1992). The mixed results found in the current study failed to make sense of this hodgepodge of previous research.

Individual differences in processing styles, as measured by the Rational-Experiential Inventory (REI), produced an interesting mix of findings. The REI consisted of two sub-scales, the Faith in Intuition (FI) scale and the Need For Cognition (NFC) scale, neither of which predicted verdict confidence scores in either study. Further, neither study found any interactions between these scales and the case type variable, indicating that FI and NFC scores did not affect participants' ability to weigh aggravators and mitigators. Although participants differed in processing style, this did not affect their ability to make decisions in a proper manner.

Though FI and NFC scores did not affect verdict confidence scores, these scores were related to a variety of other dependent measures. Rational thinkers (i.e., participants with high NFC scores) placed more responsibility on jurors (Study One), judge's instructions/state law (both studies), and the defendant (Study Two), than less rational thinkers (i.e., participants with low NFC scores). Rational thinkers also placed less responsibility on the victim (both studies), Biblical authority (Study Two), and chance (Study Two) than less rational thinkers.

Additionally, rational thinkers were more influenced by the evidence (both studies), judges' instructions (Study Two), and logic and reason[9] than less rational thinkers. Rational thinkers (i.e., high NFC scores) were less influence by Biblical authority (both studies), instincts,[10] and feelings about the defendant.[11] These results support the general notion that participants who are high in NFC make decisions in ways that are consistent with those of a "rational" juror (e.g., relying on the evidence rather than extralegal sources such as the Bible).

---

[9] This question was asked only in Study Two
[10] This question was asked only in Study Two
[11] This question was asked only in Study Two

Finally, Study Two revealed that participants with high FI scores (i.e., experiential thinkers) were more likely than those with low FI scores to be influenced by feelings about the case, feelings about the defendant and instincts about the case. Thus, the participants' processing style played an important role in decision-making, even though processing style did not affect the final verdict confidence score.

## LIMITATIONS AND FUTURE DIRECTIONS

One important limitation of this study involves the relatively sterile nature of the trial summary. Future studies should employ more realistic appeals (e.g., video taped trials) instead of the short written summary used in the present studies. An actor in a video would likely be able to deliver a more emotion-provoking appeal than is possible in a written summary. As some research (Bornstein, 1999) has indicated that more realistic simulations do not generally produce different outcomes than simple written summaries, this suggestion may not improve the results found here.

It is also possible that the manipulations that were used were not strong enough to affect participants' decision-making. The manipulation checks in Study Two revealed that many participants were not aware of the appeals or directives they had read. A more dramatic presentation may be more salient to participants. For example, the attorney could read the quotes out of a real Bible to illustrate the religious points s/he was making and use theatrical-like techniques to better capture the jurors' attentions. Stronger manipulations delivered in a more realistic manner (e.g., by a real actor rather than a written summary) may be more successful at affecting decision-making.

A second limitation involves the participants used in this study. The participants were not actual jurors; they were students and community members who were asked to pretend to be jurors in a mock trial. Although attempts were made to involve older participants, the mean age of participants was 28 in Study One and 26 in Study Two. The average age of actual juries would likely be older than the participants in these studies. While the generalizability of the sample is a concern, some research has indicated that studies using student samples may not be significantly different from studies using samples of community members (Bornstein, 1999). This may be the case in the current study, as the community members did not differ from students in many ways (e.g., verdicts). It would be difficult to study jurors in real trials using religious appeals, but it would be possible to conduct future studies using a sample of individuals who are more representative of real juries.

Further, it is impossible to fully replicate the gravity of the task of sentencing a defendant in a death penalty trial. A simple, hour-long study cannot approximate the complexity or emotional content of a real death penalty trial. Actual jurors in a real trial with real consequences may act significantly different than participants in this study.

Several studies have indicated that the decision-making processes and outcomes are different for participants who know that their decisions will have no "real life" consequence, and participants who believe that their decisions will affect real individuals (Diamond & Zeisel, 1974; Kaplan & Krupa, 1986; Wilson & Donnerstein, 1977). For example, Wilson and Donnerstein found that jurors who were told that their decisions would have real consequences arrived at significantly more guilty verdicts and recalled more of the trial evidence than participants who were told that the study was just an experiment with no real consequences (Wilson & Donnerstein, 1977). Because it is ethically impossible to conduct an experimental study in actual death penalty trials, this is a limitation that is difficult to overcome.

Finally, participants were not asked to deliberate with other people in order to come to a sentencing decision. Deliberation may affect sentencing decisions, as participants may be influenced by the opinions of other participants. Future studies should ask participants to deliberate their verdicts with other participants.

In sum, the current study had a number of limitations, some which were necessitated by the nature of the study (i.e., death penalty). Others, however, could be addressed through future studies.

# CHAPTER 12

# Conclusions

Some courts have expressed concern that religious appeals improperly affect the ability of jurors to make legally permissible sentencing decisions and reduce jurors' perceptions of personal responsibility for the sentencing decision. These initial studies indicate that religious appeals did not affect participants' abilities to weigh aggravators and mitigators, nor did they reduce perceived responsibility for the sentencing decision. Thus, it appears that the concern over the use of religious appeals may be unfounded.

It is interesting, however, that reliance on Biblical authority was related to some undesirable outcomes. For example, the more participants relied on Biblical authority, the more they also relied on their instincts and the less they relied on the evidence and judge's instructions in making their sentencing decision. Although religious appeals did not affect actual verdicts, reliance on Biblical authority may still pose a threat to proper juror decision-making, as it is associated with less reliance on legal factors such as judge's instructions. Thus, it may still be a legitimate concern that lawyers encourage jurors to rely on Biblical authority, though it is doubtful that the results found here would prompt a wide-spread ban on religious appeals.

Cognitive-Experiential Self-Theory did not prove to be a useful tool for explaining decision-making in this context. Neither appeals nor directives affected answers on the CEST measures. There are many explanations as to why the CEST measures were unsuccessful. For example, the long delay between the directive and the CEST measures may have washed out any effect. Additionally, the appeals used in these studies may not have been strong enough to trigger experiential processing. It is possible that the CEST measures do not generalize outside of the specific context used in the Epstein (1992, 1996) studies. Since the results of these findings question the validity of the CEST theory, further research is needed to determine the reasons why the directives and appeals did not affect CEST processing.

These studies revealed some individual differences. Gender, devotionalism, belief in a literal interpretation of the Bible, and an individual's usual processing style may all affect decision-making. Because some of the individual difference results (e.g., gender and devotionalism) were only found in one of the two studies, further research is needed to fully explore these relationships.

In a real trial setting, with a real defendant, a real lawyer, and real consequences, jurors may act differently than in this mock trial experiment. Further tests should be conducted in order to adequately inform judges and policymakers about the effects of religious appeals on jury decision-making.

In sum, the results of these two studies indicate that religious appeals do not interfere with jurors' sentencing decisions. Appeals did not affect verdicts or jurors' ability to weigh aggravators and mitigators properly. Nor did they affect jurors' sense of personal responsibility. Although further research will help solidify these conclusions, these initial studies indicate that religious appeals are not a threat to proper jury decision-making.

Although the studies presented in the previous chapters investigated the effects of religious appeals in closing arguments of death penalty trials, many uses of religion remain unstudied. For instance, much research needs to be conducted to determine if religious evidence (e.g., conversion to Christianity) impacts juror decisions. As the current studies only addressed the use of religion in death penalty sentencing trials, future studies should be conducted to determine whether religious instructions affect other types of trials. Studies could also be conducted to determine how jurors make decisions about a defendant's sanity or competency to stand trial based on the defendant's religious delusions or beliefs. As these examples demonstrate, most uses of religion in the criminal justice system are yet to be studied. It is hoped that the studies presented here are but the first in a long line of studies researching the effects of religion in the criminal justice system.

# References


ABA Standards for Criminal Justice 3-5.8(a) and 4-7.7(a) (3rd Ed. 1993).

Able, C. (2003, Oct 9). Juror 'rulebook' raises alarm. *Rocky Mountain News*. Retrieved November 30, 2003, from http://www.rocky mountainnews.com/drmn/local/article/0,1299,DRMN_15_2333436 ,00.html

Applegate, B. K., Cullen, F. T., Fisher, B. S., Vander Ven, T. (2000). Forgiveness and fundamentalism: Reconsidering the relationship between correctional attitudes and religion. *Criminology, 38*, 719-753.

Associated Press (2005, February 15), Severed-Arm Baby Mom Said Incompetent. Retrieved November 29, 2005, from http://www. foxnews.com/story0,2933,147633,00.html

Associated Press (2005, May 31). Judge gives offenders option of church. Retrieved November 29, 2005, from http://www.boston. com/news/nation/articles/2005/05/31/judge_gives_offenders_optio n_of_church/?rss_id=Boston.com+/+News

Associated Press (2005, June 22). Mel Gibson Stalker Sentenced. Retrieved November 29, 2005, from http://www.cbsnews.com/ stories/2005/06/22entertainment/main703561.shtml

Associated Press (2005, July 18), Eric Rudolph Gets Life Without Parole. Retrieved November 29, 2005, from http://www. foxnews.com/story/0,2933,162790,00.html

Associated Press (2005, July 27). Non-Christian texts sought for courtroom oaths. Retrieved August 1, 2005, from http://www. cnn.com/2005/law/07/27/quran.courtoom.ap/index.html

Bader, C. G. (2003). Forgive me victim for I have sinned: Why repentance and the criminal justice system do not mix—A lesson from Jewish Law. *Fordham Urban Law Journal, 31*, 69-97

Bailey, E. (2005, June 30). Church Settles Priest Abuse Claims, *LA Times*. B1.

Berg, T. C. & Ross, W. G. (1998). Some religiously devout justices: Historical notes and comments. *Marquette Law Review, 81*, 383-409.

Bjarnason, T. & Welch, M. R. (2004) Father knows best: Parishes, priests, and American Catholic parishioners' attitudes toward capital punishment. *Journal for the Scientific Study of Religion, 43*, 103-119.

Blum, V. (2005, July 8). Putting Islam on the Stand. *Law.com*. Retrieved November 29, 2005, from http://www.law.com/jsp/article.jsp?id=1120727114514

Blume, J. H., & Johnson, S. L. (2000). Don't take his eye, don't take his tooth, and don't cast the first stone: Limiting religious arguments in capital cases. *William and Mary Bill of Rights Journal, 9*, 61-104.

Bornstein, B. H. (1999). The ecological validity of jury simulations: Is the jury still out? *Law and Human Behavior, 23*, 75-91.

Bornstein, B. H. (2004). The impact of different types of expert scientific testimony on mock jurors' liability verdicts. *Psychology, Crime & Law, 10*, 429-446.

Bornstein, B. H. & Miller, M. K. (2005). Does Religion Predict Juror Decisions? *American Psychology Association Monitor, 36*, 92-3.

Brooks, E.A. (1999). Thou shalt not quote the Bible: Determining the propriety of attorney use of religious philosophy and themes in oral arguments. *Georgia Law Review, 33*, 1113-1180.

Burritt, C. (1995, July 30). Seeking meaning in Smith tragedy: Faith helps ease pain but "the mystery is why God allows certain things to happen." *Atlanta Journal and Constitution*, A 12.

Carter, S. L. (1989). The religiously devout judge. *Notre Dame Law Review, 64*, 932-943.

CNN.com (no date). The case of the Taliban American, *CNN.com*. Retrieved November 29, 2005, from http://www.cnn.com/CNN/Programs/people/shows/walker/profile.html

CNN.com (2002, March 13). Yates found guilty of murdering her children. *CNN.com*. Retrieved March 13, 2002, from http://www.cnn.com/2002/law/03/13/yates.trial/index.html

CNN.com (2002, October 24). Muhammad a Gulf War Vet, Islam Convert: Ex-wife Described as 'In Shock' over Muhammad's Arrest. *CNN.com*. Retrieved November 29, 2005, from http://archives.cnn.com/2002/US/10/24/muhammad.profile/index.html

CNN.com (2003, October 20). Kobe Bryant Must Stand Trial, Judge Rules: If Convicted, He Faces Maximum Sentence of Life in Prison, *CNN.com*. Retrieved November 29, 2005, from http://www.cnn.com/2003/LAW/10/20/bryant.hearing/index.html

CNN.com (2003, November 11). Malvo Defense Subpoenas Muhammad: Pool of Potential Jurors Winnowed to 28. *CNN.com.* Retrieved November 29, 2005, from http://www.cnn.com/2003/LAW/11/11/malvo.trial/index.html

CNN.com (2004, June 12). Juror: Sympathy Spared Nichols. *CNN.com.* Retrieved November 29, 2005, from http://www.cnn.com/2004/LAW/06/12/nichols.react/index.html

CNN.com, (2005, March 21). Ex-prosecutor says he kept Jews off juries. Cnn.com. Retrieved April 30, 2005, from http://www.cnn.com/2005/LAW/03/21/jurors.ethnicity.ap/index.html.

CNN.com (2005, April 8). Rudolph Agrees to Plea Agreement: Deal Would Allow Accused Bomber to Avoid Death Penalty. *CNN.com.* Retrieved November 29, 2005, from http://www.cnn.com/2005/LAW/04/08/rudolph.plea/index.html

CNN.com (2005, June 22). Former Klansman Found Guilty of Manslaughter: Conviction Coincides with 41st Anniversary of Civil Rights Killings. *CNN.com* Retrieved November 29, 2005, from http://www.cnn.com/2005/LAW/06/21/mississippi.killings/index.html

CNN.com (2005, June 28). Rader Details How He Killed 10 People: Killer Had 'Sexual Fantasies' While Picking Victims. *CNN.com.* Retrieved November 29, 2005, from http://www.cnn.com/2005/LAW/06/27/btk/index.html

CNN.com (2005, July 26). Smart's Accused Kidnapper Ruled Incompetent: Judge Orders Man Confined for Mental Treatment. *CNN.com* Retrieved November 29, 2005, from http://edition.cnn.com/2005/LAW/07/26/smart.suspect

CNN.com (2005, October 12). White House defends talk of Miers' religion. *CNN.com.* Retrieved November 15, 2005, from http://www.cnn.com/2005/POLITICS/10/12/miers.religion/index.html

CNN.com (2005, November 29). Governor spares convicted murderer. *CNN.com.* Retrieved Nov 29, 2005 from www.cnn.com/2005/LAW/11/29/landmark.execution.ap/index.html

Collett, T. S. (2000). The King's servant, but God's first. *South Texas Law Review, 41,* 1277-1297.

Conkle, D. O. (1998). Religiously devout judges: Issues of personal integrity and public benefit. *Marquette Law Review, 81,* 523-531.

Deutsch, L. (2004, November 2) Questionnaires Used to Reduce Jury Pool in Robert Blake Case. *North County Times*. Retrieved November 29, 2005, from  http://www.nctimes.com/articles/2004/11/03/news/state/20_18_3211_2_04.txt

DeWitt, J.S., Richardson, J.T., & Warner, L.G. (1997). Novel scientific evidence and controversial cases: A social psychological examination. *Law and Psychology Review, 21*, 1-27.

Diamond, S. S., Zeisel, H. (1974). A courtroom experiment on juror selection and decision making. *Personality and Social Psychology Bulletin, 1*, 276-277.

Dorf, M. C. (2005, April 27). Why Al Qaeda Conspirator Zacarias Moussaoui's Guilty Plea Probably Won't Save His Life, *FindLaw.com*. Retrieved November 29, 2005, from http://writ.news.findlaw.com/dorf/20050427.html

Duffy, B. C. (1997). Prosecutors' use of religious arguments in the sentencing phase of capital cases. *Vanderbilt Law Review, 50*, 1335-1385.

Echols, M. (2005). Is the courtroom the right place for religion? Difficulties in restricting religious arguments during the sentencing phase of Pennsylvania death penalty cases: Commonwealth v. Spotz. *University of West Los Angeles Law Review, 36*, 254-269.

Egland, T. T. (2004). Prejudiced by the presence of God: Keeping religious material out of death penalty deliberations. *Capital Defense Journal, 16*, 337-366.

Epstein, S., (1990). *Cognitive-Experiental Self-Theory*. Handbook of Personality: Theory & Research, NY: Guilford Press.

Epstein, S., (1994). Integration of the Cognitive and the Psychodynamic Unconscious. *American Psychologist, 49*, 709-724.

Epstein, S., Lipson, A., Holstein, C., & Huh, E. (1992). Irrational reactions to negative outcomes: Evidence for two conceptual systems. *Journal of Personality and Social Psychology, 62*, 328-339.

Epstein, S., Pacini, R., Denes-Raj, V.,  Heier, H. (1996). Individual differences in intuitive-experiential and analytical-rational thinking styles. *Journal of Personality and Social Psychology, 71*, 390-405.

Evans, T. D & Adams, M. (2003). Salvation or damnation?: Religion and correctional ideology. *American Journal of Criminal Justice, 28*, 15-36.

Flock, J. (2003, January 11). 'Blanket commutation' empties Illinois death row. *CNN.com*. Retrieved November 15, 2005, from http://www.cnn.com/2003/LAW/01/11/illinois.death.row/

Fulero, S. M. & Penrod, S. D. (1990). The myths and realties of attorney jury selection folklore and scientific jury selection: What works? *Ohio Northern University Law Review, 17*, 229-253.

Furman, H. P. (1995). Avoiding error in closing argument. *Colorado Lawyer, 24*, 33-42.

Gallup, G. The Gallup poll: Public opinion, 1995.

Garvey, J. H. & Coney, A. B (1998). Catholic judges in capital cases. *Marquette Law Review, 81*, 303-341.

Glasgow, G., & Rutchick, A. M. (2005). Priming at the polls: Can polling place location influence voting behavior? Paper presented at the annual conference of the Midwest Political Science Association, Chicago.

Gonzalez-Perez, M. (2001) A Model of Decisionmaking in Capital Juries. *International Social Science Review, 76*, 79-91.

Gorman, B. (July 2, 2004). Islam: Fastest-Growing religion among inmates. *The Brockville Recorder & Times*. E10.

Grasmick, H. G., Cochran, J. K., Bursik, R. J. Jr., & Kimpel, M. L. (1993). Religion, punitive justice and support for the death penalty. *Justice Quarterly, 10*, 289-314.

Grasmick, H. G., Davenport, E., Chamlin, M. G. & Bursik, R. J. Jr. (1992). Protestant fundamentalism and the retributive doctrine of punishment. *Criminology, 30*, 21-45.

Graziano, S.J., Panter, A.T., & Tanaka, J. S. (1990). Individual differences in information processing strategies and their role in juror decision making and selection. *Forensic Reports, 3*, 279-301.

Greenlee, M. B. (2000). Faith on the bench: The role of religious belief in the criminal sentencing decisions of judges. *University of Dayton Law Review, 26*, 1-34.

Greer, T., Berman, M., Varan, V., Bobrycki, L., & Watson, S. (2005). We are a religious people; We are a vengeful people. *Journal for the Scientific Study of Religion, 44*, 45-57.

Griffen, W. L. (1998). The case for religious values in judicial decision-making. *Marquette Law Review, 81*, 513-519.

Grinberg, E. (2005, July 15). Teens in Satanist Case Enter Plea, *CNN.com*. Retrieved November 29, 2005, from http://www.cnn.com/2005/LAW/07/15/ctv.satanist.case/index.html

Hiers, R. H. (2004). The death penalty and due process in Biblical law. *University of Detroit Mercy Law Review, 81*, 751-832.

Henson, M. (2001) Carruthers v. State: Thou shalt not make direct religious references in closing arguments. *Mercer Law Review, 52*, 731-744.

Howard, W. G., & Redfering, D. (1983) The dynamics of jury decision-making: A case study. *Social Behavior and Personality, 11*, 83-89.

Hylton, J. G. (1998). David Josiah Brewer and the Christian Constitution. *Marquette Law Review, 81*, 417.

Idleman, S.C. (1998). The limits of religious values in judicial decision making. *Marquette Law Review, 81*, 537-565.

Johnson, S. D. (1985). Religion as a defense in a mock-jury trial. *The Journal of Social Psychology, 125*, 213-220.

Kaplan, M. F., & S. Krupa, S. (1986). Severe penalties under the control of others can reduce guilt verdicts. *Law and Psychology Review, 10*, 1-18.

Kershaw, Sarah (2002, November 21). Jury is begged to spare the Wendy's Killer. New York Times. Retrieved November 21, 2002, from http://www.nytimes.com/2002/11/21/nyregion/21Wend. html?ex=1039938855&ei=1&en=54ac2d3804cf6878

Kerr, N. L., Hymes, R. W., Anderson, A. B., & Weathers, J. E. (1995) Defendant-juror similarity and mock juror judgments. *Law and Human Behavior, 19*, 545-567.

Lassiter, G.D., Slaw, R.D., Briggs, M.A. & Scanlan, C.R. (1992). The potential for bias in videotaped confessions. *Journal of Applied Social Psychology, 22*, 1838-1851.

Leiber, M.J., & Woodrick, A.C. (1997). Religious beliefs, attributional styles, and adherence to correctional orientation. *Criminal Justice and Behavior, 24*, 495-511.

Lesnick, H. (2002). No other Gods: Answering the call of faith in the practice of law. *Journal of Law and Religion, 18*, 459-485.

Lester, D., Maggioncalda-Aretz, M. , Stark, S. H. (1997). Adolescents' attitudes toward the death penalty. *Adolescence, 32*, 447-449.

Lindsay, S. (2003, May 24). Harlan's sentence tossed: Killer's death penalty thrown out because jurors used Bible. *Rocky Mountain News*, p. 4A.

Loewy, A. H. (2000). Religious neutrality and the death penalty. *William and Mary Bill of Rights Journal, 9*, 191-200.

Maimon, A. (2005, May 31). Judge lets some defendants attend worship as sentencing option. *The Courier-Journal*. Retrieved November 29, 2005 from http://www.courier-journal.com/apps/pbcs.dll/article?AID=/20050531/NEWS0104/505310376/1008/NEWS01

Mansfield, J. H. (2004). Peremptory challenges to jurors based upon or affecting religion. *Seaton Hall Law Review, 34*, 435-473.

Menon, V. (July 7, 2004). Rise of Islam in jails a risk? *Toronto Star*, F 01.

Miller, M. K. & Bornstein, B. H. (2005). Religious Appeals in Closing Arguments: Impermissible Input or Benign Banter? *Law and Psychology Review, 29*, 29-61.

Miller, M. K. & Hayward, R. D. (under review). Using Peremptory Challenges to Remove Potential Jurors Based on their Religion: Commonsense or Nonsense?

Miller, M.K., Singer, J. & Jehle, A. (2005). Religion in the courts: A psychological analysis of the role of religious attitudes in legal decision-making. Unpublished manuscript.

Modka-Truran, M. C. (2004). Reenchanting the law: The religious dimension of judicial decision making. *Catholic University Law Review, 53*, 709- 800.

Montz, C. L. (2001). Why lawyers continue to cross the line in closing arguments: Examination of federal and state cases. *Ohio Northern University Law Review, 28*, 67-131.

Morganthau, T. (1995, August 7). Smith condemned to life, *Newsweek*, at 19.

O'Neil, K. M., Patry, M.W., & Penrod, S.D. (2004). Exploring the effects of attitudes toward the death penalty on capital sentencing verdicts. *Psychology, Public Policy, and Law, 10*, 443-470.

Osler, M. (2005). The lawyer's humble walk. *Pepperdine Law Review, 32*, 483-496.

Pankratz, H. (2005). U.S. Supreme Court allows ruling on Bible in jurors' room to stand. *Denver Post*, p. B-02.

Paulson, S. K. (2005, March 29). Colorado Supreme Court throws out Bible-reading jurors' death sentence. Associated Press. Retrieved November 10, 2005, from http://www.law.com/jsp/article.jsp?id=1112016916928

Pearce, R. G. & Uelmen, A. J. (2004). Religious lawyering in a liberal democracy: A challenge and an invitation. *Case Western Reserve Law Review, 55*, 127-161.

Pennington, N., & Hastie, R. (1986). Evidence evaluation in complex decision-making. *Journal of Personality and Social Psychology, 51,* 242-258.

Pennington, N., & Hastie, R. (1988). Explanation-based decision making: Effects of memory structure on judgment. *Journal of Experimental Psychology: Learning, Memory, and Cognition. 14,* 521-533.

Polk, J. (2004, June 7). Nichols More Committed to Religion, Sister Testifies: Defense Argues to Save Bombing Conspirator's Life, *CNN.com.* Retrieved November 29, 2005, from http://www.cnn.com/2004/LAW/06/07/nichols.trial/index.html.

Putney, S., & Middleton, R. (1961). Dimensions and correlates of religious ideologies. *Social Forces, 39,* 285-290.

Reid, C. J. (2004).  The unavoidable influence of religion upon the law of marriage. *Quinnipiac Law Review, 23,* 493-521.

Ryan,  H. (2004, April 1). Williams Will Not Testify: Attorneys for Ex-NBA Star Rest Case. *CNN.com.* Retrieved  November 29, 2005 from http://www.cnn.com/2004/LAW/04/01/jayson.williams/index.html

Richardson, J. T. & Introvigne, M. (2001). "Brainwashing" theories in European Parliamentary and Administrative Reports on "cults" and "sects." *Journal for the Scientific Study of Religion, 40,* 143-168.

Sandys, M. & McGarrell, E. F. (1995). Attitudes toward capital punishment: Preference for the penalty or mere acceptance? *Journal of Research in Crime and Delinquency, 32,* 191-213.

Seper, J. (May 6, 2004). Prisons breeding ground for terror? *Washington Times*, A11.

Shenai Raif & Neville Dean, *Repentant Shoebomber Jailed for 13 Years*, Press Association (Apr. 22, 2005).

Simmonds, A. R. (2004). Measure for measure: Two misunderstood principles of damages, Exodus 21:22-25, "Life for life, eye for eye," and Matthew 5:38-39, "Turn the other cheek." *St. Thomas Law Review, 17,* 123-171

Simons, M. A. (2004). Born again on death row: Retribution, remorse, and religion. *The Catholic Lawyer,* 311-336.

Simson, G. J. & Garvey, S. P. (2001) Knockin' on heaven's door: Rethinking the role of religion in death penalty cases. *Cornell Law Review, 86,* 1090-1130

Sisk, G. C., Heise, M., & Morriss, A. P. (2004). Searching for the soul of judicial decisionmaking: An empirical study of religious freedom decisions. *Ohio State Law Journal, 65,* 491- 594.

Songer, D. R. & Tabrizi, S. J. (2000). The religious right in court: The decision making of Christian evangelicals in state supreme courts. *The Journal of Politics, 61*, 507-26.

Sweetingham, L. (2005, March 1). Alone at the Defense Table, Accused Mel Gibson Stalker Picks Jury. *CNN.com*. Retrieved November 29, 2005, from http://www.cnn.com/2005/LAW/03/01/sinclair/index.html

Springer, J. (2004, April 5). Jury Accepts Insanity Defense for Mother Who Stoned Sons, Court TV. Retrieved November 29, 2005, from http://www.courttv.com/trials/laney/040304_verdict_ctv.html

Smith, S. D. (1998). Legal Discourse and The De Facto Disestablishment. *Marquette Law Review, 81*, 203-213.

Smith, C. S. (2004) Growing Muslim prison population poses huge risks: France's struggle with radical Islam. *New York Times*, p. 1.

Tversky, A., & Kahneman, D. (1974). Judgment under uncertainty: Heuristics and biases. *Science, 185*, 1124-1131.

U.S. v. Nichols, 96-CR-68, United States District Court for the District of Colorado (Oct. 30, 1997) Reporter's Transcript, Trial to Jury: Vol. 53. Retrieved November 29, 2005, from http://www.courttv.com/archive/casefiles/oklahoma/nichtranscripts/1030am.html

Valliant, P.M. & Oliver, C.L. (1997). Attitudes toward capital punishment: A function of leadership style, gender and personality. *Social Behavior & Personality, 25*, 161-168.

Vogel, B. (2003). Support for life in prison without the possibility of parole among death penalty proponents. *American Journal of Criminal Justice, 27*, 263-275.

Waggoner, C. A. (2004). Peremptory challenges and religion: The unanswered prayer for a Supreme Court Opinion. *Loyola University of Chicago Law Journal, 36*, 285-328.

Walker, A. D. (2003). "The murderer shall surely be put to death:" The impropriety of Biblical arguments in the penalty phase of capital cases. *Washburn Law Journal, 43*, 197-225.

Whitehead, J.T & Blankenship, M.B. (2000). The gender gap in capital punishment attitudes: An analysis of support and opposition. *American Journal of Criminal Justice, 25*, 1-12.

Wilson, D.W., & Donnerstein, E. (1977). Guilty or not guilty? A look at the "simulated" jury paradigm. *Journal of Applied Social Psychology, 7*, 175-190.

Wiehl, L. (2000). Judges and lawyers are not singing from the same hymnal when it comes to allowing the Bible in the courtroom. *American Journal of Trial Advocacy, 24*, 273-296.

Young, R. L. (1992). Religious orientation, race and support for the death penalty. *Journal for the Scientific Study of Religion, 31*, 76-88.

Zoll, R. (2005, June 4). American prisons become political, religious battleground. *SignOnSanDiego.com*. Retrieved November 29, 2005, from http://www.signonsandiego.com/news/nation/20050604-0928-struggleforislamii.html

# Cases Cited

*Batson v. Kentucky*, 476 U.S. 79 (1986)
*Bennett v. Angelone*, 92 F.3d 1336 (Va. 1996)
*Berry v. State,* 703 So. 2d 269 (Miss. 1997)
*Boyd v. French*, 147 F.3d 319 (N.C. 1998)
*Bowers v Hardwick*, 478 U.S. 186 (1986).
*Bracy v. Gramley*, 81 F. 3d 684 (Ill. 1996)
*Brown v. Payton*, 125 S. Ct. 1432 (2005)
*Bussard v. Lockhart*, 32 F.3d 322 (Ark. 1994)
*Buttrum v. Black*, 721 F.Supp. 1268 (Ga. 1989)
*Caldwell v. Mississippi*, 472 U.S. 320 (1985)
*Carruthers v. State*, 528 S.E.2d 217 (Ga. 2000)
*Casarez v. State*, 913 S.W.2d 468 (Tex. 1995)
*Chapman v. California,* 87 S.Ct. 824 (Cal. 1967)
*Christeson v. State*, 131 S.W.3d 796 (Mo.,2004)
*Coe v. Bell*, 161 F.3d 320 (Tenn. 1998)
*Cole v. State*, 584 S.E.2d 37 (Ga. 2003)
*Colorado v. Harlan*, 126 S.Ct. 399 (2005)
*Commonwealth v. Brown*, 711 A.2d 444 (Pa. 1998)
*Commonwealth v. Chambers*, 599 A.2d 630 (Pa. 1991)
*Commonwealth v. Cook*, 676 A.2d 639, 649 (Pa. 1996)
*Commonwealth v. Daniels*, 644 A.2d 1175 (Pa. 1994)
*Commonwealth v. DeJesus*, WL 2363726 (Pa. 2004)
*Commonwealth v. Henry*, 569 A.2d 929 (Pa. 1990)
*Commonwealth v. Spotz*, 756 A.2d 1139 (Pa. 2000)
*Commonwealth v. Whitney*, 512 A.2d 1152 (Pa. 1986)
*Cunningham v. Zant*, 928 F.2d 1006 (Ga. 1991)
*Crowe v. State*, 458 S.E. 2d, 799 (Ga. 1995)
*Daniels v. Lee*, 316 F.3d 477 (N.C. 2003)
*Daniels v. North Carolina*, 115 S.Ct. 953 (1995)
*Davis v. Minnesota*, 511 U.S. 1115 (1994)
*Donnelly v. DeChristoforo*, 94 S. Ct. 1868 (1974)
*Doss v. State*, 709 So. 2d 369 (Miss. 1996)
*Eldred v. Commonwealth*, 906 S.W.2d 694 (Ky. 1994)
*Ex parte Waldrop*, 459 So. 2d 959 (Ala. 1984)
*Furman v. Georgia*, 408 U.S. 238 (1972)
*Gibson v. State*, 501 P.2d 891 (Okla. 1972)
*Godfrey v. Georgia*, 446 U.S. 420 (1980)
*Greene v. State*, 469 S.E.2d 129 (Ga. 1996)

*Gregg v. Georgia*, 96 S.Ct. 2909 (1976)
*Hammond v. State*, 452 S.E.2d 745 (Ga. 1995)
*Hill v. State*, 427 S.E.2d 770 (Ga. 1993)
*Ice v. Commonwealth*, 667 S.W.2d 671 (Ky. 1984)
*Jones v. Kemp*, 706 F.Supp. 1534 (Ga. 1989)
*La Rocca v. Lane*, 47 A.D.2d 243 (1975)
*Lewis v. State*, 592 S.E.2d 405 (Ga. 2004)
*Lockett v. Ohio*, 438 U.S. 586 (1978)
*Long v. State*, 883 P.2d 167 (Okla. 1972)
*McNair v. State*, 653 So. 2d 320 (Ala. 1992)
*Miller v. North Carolina*, 583 F.2d 701 (N.C. 1978)
*Miniel v. Cockrell*, 339 F. 3d 331 (Tex. 2003)
*Minnesota v. Davis*, 504 N.W.2d 767 (Minn. 1993)
*Payne v. Tennessee*, 111 S. Ct. 2597 (1991)
*People v. Bradford*, 929 P.2d 544 (Cal. 1997)
*People v. Clark*, 857 P.2d 1099 (Cal. 1993)
*People v. Davenport*, 906 P.2d 1068 (Cal. 1996)
*People v. Eckles*, 404 N.E.2d 358 (Ill. 1980)
*People v. Freeman*, 882 P.2d 249 (Cal. 1994)
*People v. Harrison*, 25 Cal. Rptr. 3d. 224 (Cal. 2005)
*People v. Hill*, 839 P.2d 984 (Cal. 1992)
*People v. Jackson*, 920 P.2d 1254 (Cal. 1996)
*People v. Mahaffey*, 651 N.E.2d 1055 (Ill. 1995)
*People v. Martin*, 64 Cal. App. 4th 378. (Cal. 1998)
*People v. Morgan*, 187 Ill.2d 500 (Ill. 1999)
*People v. Payton*, 839 P.2d 1035 (Cal. 1992)
*People v. Pizzaro*, 7 A.D.3d 395, (N.Y. 2004)
*People v. Rohn*, 296 N.W.2d 315 (Mich. 1980)
*People v. Sandoval*, 841 P.2d 862 (Cal. 1992)
*People v. Wash*, 861 P.2d 1107 (Cal. 1993)
*People v. Wolley*, 205 Ill. 2d 296 (Ill. 202)
*People v. Wrest*, 839 P.2d 1020, 1028 (Cal. 1992)
*Robinson v. State*, 900 P.2d 389 (Okla. 1995)
*Sandoval v. Calderon*, 241 F.3d 765, 777 (Cal. 2000)
*Shell v. State*, 554 So. 2d 887 (Miss. 1989)
*State v. Alston*, 461 S.E.2d 687 (N.C. 1995)
*State v. Arnett*, 724 N.E.2d 793 (Ohio 2000)
*State v. Artis*, 384 S.E.2d 470, 500 (N.C. 1989)
*State v. Cauthern*, 1996 WL 937660 (Tenn. 1996)
*State v. Ceballos*, 832 A. 2d 14, (Conn. 2003)
*State v. Cribbs* 967 S. W. 2d 773 (Tenn. 1998)

*State v. Daniels*, 446 S.E.2d 298, 320 (N.C. 1994)
*State v. Debler*, 856 S.W.2d 641 (Mo. 1993)
*State v. Eaton*, 445 S.E. 2d 917 (N.C. 1994)
*State v. Fuller*, 862 A.2d 1130 (N.J. 2004)
*State v. Fullwood*, 373 S. E. 2d 518 (N. C. 1988)
*State v. Gentry*, 888 P. 2d. 1105 (Wash. 1995)
*State v. Gibbs*, 436 S.E.2d 321 (N.C. 1993)
*State v. Haselden*, 577 S.E.2d 594 (N.C. 2003)
*State v. Hatcher*, WL 2058909 (Tenn. 2004)
*State v. Hodge*, 726 A.2d 531 (Conn. 1999)
*State v. Holden*, 488 S.E.2d 514 (N.C. 1997)
*State v. Holmes*, 824 N.E.2d 562 (Ohio 2005)
*State v. Lundgren*, 653 N.E. 2d 304 (Ohio, 1995)
*State v. Messiah*, 538 So. 2d 175 (La. 1988)
*State v. McCary*, 119 S.W.3d 226 (Tenn. 2003)
*State v. Middlebrooks*, 995 S.W.2d 550 (Tenn. 1999)
*State v. Moose*, 313 S.E.2d 507, 519 (S.C. 1984)
*State v. Murphy*, 747 N.E.2d 765 (Ohio 2001)
*State v. Patterson*, 482 S.E.2d 760 (S.C. 1996)
*State v. Phillips*, 940 S.W.2d 512 (Mo. 1997)
*State v. Purcell*, 18 P.3d 113 (Ariz. 2001)
*State v. Ramsey*, 864 S.W. 320 (Mo. 1993)
*State v. Richardson*, 995 S.W. 2d 119 (Tenn. 1998)
State v. Roache, 595 S. E. 2d 381 (N.C. 2004)
*State v. Shafer*, 531 S.E.2d 524, 532 (S.C. 2000)
*State v. Shurn*, 866 S.W.2d 447 (Mo. 1993)
*State v. Sidden*, 491 S.E.2d 225 (N.C. 1997)
*State v. Thompson*, 832 A.2d 626 (Conn. 2003)
*State v. Wangberg*, 136 N.W.2d 853 (Minn. 1965)
*State v. Williams*, 510 S.E.2d 626 (N.C. 1999)
*Thompson v. State*, 581 So. 2d 1216 (Ala. 1991)
*Thornson v. State*, 721 So. 2d 590 (Miss. 1998)
*Tucker v. Zant*, 724 F. 2d 882 (Ga. 1984)
*United States v. DeJesus*, 347 F.3d 500 (N.J. 2003)
*United States v. Giry*, 818 F.2d 120 (P.R. 1987)
*United States v. Hasting*, 103 S. Ct. 1974 (1983)
*United States v. Rodriguez*, 765 F.2d 1546 (Fla. 1985)
*Wainwright v. Witt*, 469 U.S. 412 (1985)

# Appendices



APPENDIX A: CASE SUMMARY (BOTH STUDIES)

Instructions:

As a participant, you will be asked to become a juror in a death penalty trial. A previous jury found the defendant guilty of first degree murder, a crime that is eligible for the death penalty. Your task is to determine the appropriate punishment for the defendant. You will be asked to read a brief transcript of the evidence and attorney arguments presented in the trial. Then you will be asked to make a sentencing decision and answer some questions about your perceptions of the case. Please read the materials carefully and imagine that you are an actual juror in this case.

The following case facts were established during trial:

On June 17, 1998, Michael Bradley arrived at his home where his wife Miranda awaited him. The two had been having marital difficulties for quite some time, largely due to ongoing financial difficulties stemming from Michael's inability to sustain full time employment. The factory where Michael had worked for four years had recently closed, and he had been unable to find another full time job. Miranda was visibly upset and informed Michael that they had received notice that they would be evicted if they did not pay several months of past-due rent immediately. The two became involved in a heated argument which ended with Miranda telling Michael to move out of the house. Visibly upset, Michael got in his car and sped across town to the home of his aunt, Geraldine Spencer. Michael knew that Geraldine always kept a large amount of cash in her home and he hoped to borrow enough money to pay the past-due rent.

Michael told Geraldine that Miranda had kicked him out of the house and begged her to lend him money to pay rent and allow him to move in with her until he worked out his living situation. Geraldine refused to give Michael any money because he had failed to pay back previous loans. The two began arguing fiercely. Michael became enraged and punched Geraldine in the mouth and face. She fell to the floor, semi-conscious.

[High mitigators condition only: Michael wrapped an electrical cord around her neck three times, strangling her.]

[High aggravators condition only: Michael wrapped an electrical cord around her nick three times, strangling her. As she fought to free herself from the cord, Michael went to the kitchen and grabbed a butcher's knife. Michael stabbed Geraldine multiple times, leaving her on the floor in a pool of blood.]

Geraldine died from the injuries sustained during the altercation. Knowing where Geraldine kept her money, Michael took approximately $4500 and fled from the house. Michael returned to his home and was met by an angry Miranda who refused to allow him to enter the house to get some of his belongings. The couple remained in the front yard, arguing for about 10 minutes before Michael pushed Miranda to the ground and went into the garage. Michael grabbed a hammer from the garage as he entered the house thorough the garage door and proceeded to the bedroom. Miranda met him in the hallway, yelling at him to get out of the house. Michael hit Miranda in the head several times with the hammer, and she fled from the house screaming. She ran to the home of the neighbor, Joe Blake, who phoned the police. Joe then went to Michael's house to investigate. Michael swung the hammer at Joe, but missed. Michael screamed at Joe and threatened to kill him if he did not leave. Joe returned home to check on Miranda and wait for the police.

The police arrived and arrested Michael for assaulting Miranda and Joe. By this time, Michael had calmed down and was apprehended without further confrontation. Miranda was taken to the hospital, where she stayed for two days. She made a full recovery from her injuries.

[High mitigators condition only: In the car, Michael voluntarily told the police that he had killed his aunt and stolen her money. The police had not yet discovered that crime, and he freely told them all he knew. He gave the officer the directions to Geraldine's house. When they arrived, Michael led the officer to her body and showed them where the money had been hidden.]

[High aggravators condition only: The next day, Geraldine's body was found, and evidence recovered from the scene led them to believe

Michael was responsible. When confronted, Michael told the police that he had killed his aunt and stolen her money.]

[High mitigators condition only: While in prison awaiting trial, Michael was witness to a fight in which one prisoner was injured and eventually died. Michael reported the altercation to the guards, and later testified against the prisoner who had caused the injury. Michael's testimony was essential to the prosecution's case and helped secure the prisoner's conviction.]

The defense offered evidence regarding Michael's potential for rehabilitation. Michael sought out and was an active participant in counseling while in prison. He was able to make progress in coping with depression and anger management issues he has struggled with throughout most of his adult life. Various authorities testified that he has been a model prisoner and has an excellent chance of being rehabilitated with proper psychological treatment.

[High aggravators condition only: The prosecution provided evidence that Michael had previously been convicted of armed robbery of a convenience store, a felony. Michael served his sentence and was released nearly 5 years before he murdered Geraldine.]

APPENDIX B: ATTORNEY ARGUMENTS

The prosecutor presented this closing argument:

Some crimes are so terrible that the person who commits the crime should forfeit his right to expect our society to support him for the remainder of his life. The crime committed by Mr. Bradley is a crime in that category. The law recognizes that there are certain circumstances that will make a death sentence more appropriate in some cases. There are such factors present in this case. Mr. Bradley committed murder for money. He asked his aunt for money, she said no. So he killed her, just to get some money. And that wasn't enough, he continued his rampage when he got back home, and attacked his wife and neighbor with a hammer. These are the types of factors that also point toward a death sentence. You will read about them in the jury instructions. The law requires that you consider these factors, and all the other circumstances presented at trial, when you make your decision about the most appropriate sentence for Mr. Bradley. As you heard in the trial, the evidence clearly demonstrated that there are many circumstances that point to the only appropriate sentence: the death penalty.

[Study 1 only; all conditions: Your task today as jurors is to look at all the evidence and determine the appropriate sentence. How? Well, Imagine you have a scale of justice. On that scale, you will weigh all the evidence on both sides, and see which side is heavier. Is there more evidence that points to a sentence of death? Or more evidence that points to a sentence of life? That is for you to decide. I know you are probably worried about making this decision. It is a very tough decision to make, but I know you can do it.

[Study 1 only: Experiential directive: How can you possibly know how to make that decision? I'll tell you how. Read the instructions carefully, then use your gut instincts. Everyone has those "feelings" about things. Trust those feelings, those instincts as your guide. Deep down inside you is the answer. Your heart will tell you which way the scales tip. Take a look and you will find the answer within yourself.]

[Study 1 only: Rational directive: How can you possibly know how to make that decision? I'll tell you how.   Read through the jury instructions carefully, more than once if you need to. Use the instructions like a road map. Follow them closely and they will guide you through and lead you to the right answer. The answer to this decision is in the instructions. Sort of like a logic puzzle, think it through carefully, and the answer will become clear to you.]

[Study 1 only: religious appeal: While making your decision, I suggest that you think about what God has to say about people who kill. He commands us to take "an eye for an eye" and "a tooth for a tooth." This means that if someone kills someone, he or she also should be put to death. God also commanded, "He who smiteth a man, so that he die, shall be surely put to death" and "whoso sheddeth the man's blood, by man shall his blood be shed." Doesn't get much clearer than that, does it? Whoever sheds a man's blood, will have his own blood shed by man. Why does God feel so strongly about this? Because He is trying to protect His children. Because murderers rob their victims of their right to become whatever God has planned for them. Should that go unpunished? God says no.   God is very clear about the appropriate punishment for murder. An eye for an eye.   It's that simple. Mr. Bradley killed, so he should be put to death. Think of "an eye for an eye" as an equation God provides for you.   It has already been determined that Mr. Bradley killed. That half of the equation is complete. It's up to you to finish the equation. This is what retribution is about. This is what God teaches us is the right thing to do.]

[Study 1 only: non-religious appeal: While making your decision, I suggest that you think about what the law has to say about people who kill. When your scale of justice tips in favor of a death sentence, the law tells us take a life for a life. This means that, if someone kills someone, it is appropriate to put that person to death. The law also says that, if a person kills for money, that is indication that he should be put to death. If a man kills someone as part of a series of crimes, he should be put to death. Doesn't get much clearer than that, does it? Whoever kills under these circumstances, should be killed. Why does the law feel so strongly about this? Because the law is trying to protect its citizens. Because murderers rob their victims of the right to become good, productive citizens. Should that go unpunished? The law says no. The law is very clear about the appropriate punishment for murder.  When the scales of justice tip in favor of death, the murderer should die because he killed. It's that simple. Mr. Bradley killed, so he should be put to death. Think of it as an equation the law provides for you. It has already been determined that Mr. Bradley killed. That half of the equation is complete. It's up to you to finish the equation. This is what retribution is about. This is what the law teaches us is the right thing to do.]

The defense will tell you that there are things that make Mr. Bradley less blameworthy for these crimes. But I don't think there are any excuses to murder, no factor that can take away the blame. Everyone has the right to choose their actions, and everyone should take responsibility for their actions. Mr. Bradley choose to kill. I urge you not to let him shirk the responsibility for his actions. Consider all the factors of this case. Are there really any excuses that relieve the blame for Mr. Bradley' actions? No. There is nothing in the case presented by the defense that outweighs the factors that indicate that the death is the most appropriate sentence.

The defense attorney presented this closing argument:

As jurors, you have a life and death decision to make. It is a decision to be made carefully; a man's life is at stake. The law recognizes that, in some cases, there are reasons that the death penalty is not the appropriate sentence. The law requires you to consider these circumstances because these factors are how the law separates those who deserve the death penalty and those that do not. These factors are not excuses, but they are factors that reduce the defendant's moral blameworthiness and are valid reasons for allowing the defendant to live the rest of his life in prison rather than sentencing him to death. Consider the extreme psychological pressure the defendant was under. The factory where he had worked for four years closed, leaving him with no way to support his family. He had problems finding a new job, and his debt was piling up. He was going to get evicted if he didn't pay rent. His marriage was failing. Add to this the horrible fight he had with his wife, and consider that she kicked him out of her home. His marriage was over. He had lost everything. His own aunt wouldn't let him stay with her or lend him money to help his situation. In a moment of weakness, he let his temper get the best of him. He snapped. He just wanted to borrow some money, but, sorrowfully, things did not go as planned.

Although he has these tremendous psychological difficulties, he has sought counseling since then. He's made great improvements, and his doctors say he is very likely to be able to work through his depression and anger issues. He can fix what is wrong. These are the type of factors that indicate that Mr. Bradley doesn't deserve to die. The law requires that you consider these circumstances that show that the best sentence is life imprisonment.

[Study 2 only; all conditions: Your task today as jurors is to look at all the evidence and determine the appropriate sentence. How? Well, Imagine you have a scale of justice. On that scale, you will weigh all the evidence on both sides, and see which side is heavier. Is there more evidence that points to a sentence of death? Or more evidence that points to a sentence of life? That is for you to decide. I know you are probably worried about making this decision. It is a very tough decision to make, but I know you can do it.

[Study 2 only: Experiential directive: Today your task is to decide what sentence Mr. Bradley will receive. How can you possibly know how to make that decision? I'll tell you how. Read the instructions carefully, then use your gut instincts. Everyone has those "feelings" about things. Trust those feelings and your instincts as your guide. Follow your common sense and you will find the right answer. You may be confused right now, but trust in your feelings. The instructions will ask you questions, and you will simply answer "yes" or "no" and your feelings will tell you what the right answers are. You don't need anything fancy, just common sense. You don't have to worry about anything except the answers you have in your heart.
You have what it takes to find the right answers: feelings and emotions. That is all you need to know. You can think of this task as a type of test of your feelings. There is an answer deep inside you, and you have your feelings to help you find it. Apply the answers your heart gives you and think about how you feel about this. The answer will become clear to you.]

[Study 2 only: Rational directive: Today your task is to decide what sentence Mr. Bradley will receive. How can you possibly know how to make that decision? I'll tell you how. Read through the jury instructions carefully, more than once if you need to. Then use the instructions like a road map. Follow them closely and they will guide you through and lead you to the right answer. You may be confused right now, but trust in the instructions the judge will give you. They will ask you questions, and you will simply answer "yes" or "no" and the instructions will then lead you to the correct final verdict. You don't need anything fancy, just logical, dispassionate, rational thinking. Be careful that you aren't swayed by your emotions. Your duty as a juror is to decide the proper verdict based on the law, not on your emotions. You don't have to worry about anything except the logical answers to the questions in the instructions.

You have what it takes to find the right verdict: reason and logic. That is all you need to know. You can think of this task as a type of logic puzzle. There is a right answer to the puzzle, and you have the instructions to help you find it. Apply your logical reasoning and think it through carefully. The answer will become clear to you.]


[Study 2 only: religious appeal: What does God have to say about the death penalty? God has provided instructions for you to follow. The Bible says, "Vengeance is mine, thus sayeth the Lord," this means that it is not your job to decide the ultimate fate of Mr. Bradley. Throughout the Bible, God gives many examples of forgiveness. The perfect example is a quote from Jesus himself. Jesus tells us "You have heard that it has been said 'an eye for an eye and a tooth for a tooth' but I say to you, do not resist an evil doer. If someone strikes you on the right cheek, turn the other also." Jesus, the example God sent for us to follow, practiced forgiveness.

To give you an example, Jesus, who was without sin, was crucified, tortured and left to die. Yet he did not wish death upon his murderers. Jesus cried from the cross, "Forgive them Father for they know not what they do." Here's another example: In John 8, a woman is caught for adultery, a crime punishable by death. Jesus tells her would-be executioners "he that is without sin among you, let him cast the first stone." Later in the story, Jesus released the woman stating,

"Neither do I condemn you." Jesus stopped the execution in favor of mercy and forgiveness.

Turn the other cheek. Don't cast stones. Show mercy. This doesn't mean let Mr. Bradley go free, just to spare his life. I believe that you will not put Mr. Bradley to death, that you will determine that he deserves to be forgiven and that the appropriate sentence is life in prison without parole. Clearly this is the message God sends. Choose to show mercy.]


[Study 2 only: non-religious appeal: What else does the law have to say about the death penalty? The court will provide instructions for you to follow. Throughout the jury instructions, you will see there are many reasons the law gives you to forgive the defendant. Yes, there are reasons the law gives that a person might deserve the death penalty, but if you continue on, the law provides many reasons to give a life sentence in a case like this. Even though he has done wrong, he doesn't deserve to die. The law sets the example of mercy.

To give you an example, imagine that someone kills another person, an innocent person, maybe even a small child. Even if the killer tortures and kills in the cruelest way possible, the law allows you to show mercy, to spare the defendant. Even if you decide that the defendant committed the crime and there are lots of factors that tell you that he should receive the death penalty, you don't have to give the death penalty. You can still choose to give life in prison without possibility of parole. The law is very clear that you can always find that he should be shown mercy and be spared from death. The law specifically allows you to forgive.

Forgiveness. Mercy. This doesn't mean let Mr. Bradley go free, just to spare his life. I believe that you will not put Mr. Bradley to death, that you will determine that he deserves to be forgiven and that the appropriate sentence is life in prison without parole. Clearly this is the message the law sends. Choose to show mercy.]

The death penalty is reserved only for the most horrible and vicious criminals that are beyond help, and do not deserve to live. As you have seen, Mr. Bradley is not among this class of criminals. He is a loving son. A caring friend. A hard worker. Though being a good person does not give anyone the right to kill, it shows that he does not deserve to die. By giving a sentence of life imprisonment, you are not excusing what he did. You are just saying that he is not among the most awful criminals who truly are not fit to walk the earth.

## APPENDIX C: JUDGE'S INSTRUCTIONS

The judge issued the following instructions to guide your sentencing decision:

For you to recommend that the defendant be sentenced to death, a jury must decide, beyond a reasonable doubt, that the defendant is guilty of first degree murder. A reasonable doubt is a doubt based on reason and common sense, arising out of some or all of the evidence that has been presented, or lack or insufficiency of the evidence, as the case may be. Proof beyond a reasonable doubt is proof that fully satisfies or entirely convinces you that the defendant: 1) killed or attempted to kill the victim or 2) intended to kill the victim or 3) intended that deadly force would be used in the course of the felony.

The previous jury found the defendant guilty of murder in the first, and it is now your duty to recommend to the Court whether the defendant should be sentenced to death or to life imprisonment without parole. It is now your duty and ultimate responsibility to apply the law which I am about to give you concerning punishment to the case facts. It is absolutely necessary that you understand and apply the law as I give it to you, and not as you think it is, or might like it to be. This is important, because justice requires that everyone who is sentenced for first degree murder have the sentence recommendation determined in the same manner, and have the same law applied to him.

You are the sole judges of the weight to be given any evidence. By this I mean, if you decide that certain evidence is believable you must then determine the importance of that evidence in light of all other believable evidence in the case. For you to recommend that the defendant be sentenced to death, the State must prove three things beyond a reasonable doubt. Proof beyond a reasonable doubt is proof that fully satisfies or entirely convinces you of each of the following things:

First, that one or more aggravating circumstances existed; Second, that the mitigating circumstances are insufficient to outweigh any aggravating circumstances you have found. And Third, that any aggravating circumstances you have found are sufficiently substantial to call for the imposition of the death penalty when considered with any mitigating circumstances.

If you find all three of these things beyond a reasonable doubt, it would be your duty and responsibility to recommend that the defendant be sentenced to death. On the other hand, if you find that one or more of these three things has not been proven beyond a reasonable doubt, it would be your duty and responsibility to recommend that the defendant be sentenced to life imprisonment.

When you deliberate your recommendation as to punishment, you use a form entitled, "Issues and Recommendation as to Punishment." This form contains a written list of four issues, relating to aggravating and mitigating circumstances. I will now take up these four issues with you in greater detail, one by one. To enable you to follow the instructions more easily, please look at the form entitled "Issues and Recommendation as to Punishment."

Issue One is, "Do you find from the evidence, beyond a reasonable doubt, the existence of one or more of the following aggravating circumstances?" The possible aggravating circumstances are listed on the form, and you should consider each of them before you answer Issue One.

The State must prove from the evidence beyond a reasonable doubt the existence of any aggravating circumstance. An aggravating circumstance is a fact or group of facts which tend to make a specific murder particularly deserving of the maximum punishment prescribed by law. Our law identifies the aggravating circumstances which might justify a sentence of death. The following are the aggravating circumstances which might be applicable to this case.

(This aggravator only in the high aggravator condition) First, had the defendant been previously convicted of a felony involving the threat of violence to the person? Armed robbery is by definition a felony involving the threat of violence to the person. A felony involves the threat of violence to the person if the perpetrator kills or inflicts physical injury on the victim, or threatens to do so, in order to accomplish his criminal act. If you find from the evidence beyond a reasonable doubt that this aggravating circumstance exists, you would so indicate by writing, "Yes," in the space after this aggravating circumstance on the "Issues and Recommendation" form. If you do not so find, or have a reasonable doubt as to one or more of these things, you will write, "No," in that space.

Was this murder committed for pecuniary gain? A murder is committed for pecuniary gain if the defendant, when he commits it, has obtained, or intends or expects to obtain, money or some other thing which can be valued in money, either as compensation for committing it, or as a result of the death of the victim. If you find from the evidence beyond a reasonable doubt that this aggravating circumstance exists, you would so indicate by writing, "Yes," in the space after this aggravating circumstance on the "Issues and Recommendation" form. If you do not so find, or have a reasonable doubt as to one or more of these things, you will write, "No," in that space.

(This aggravator only in the high aggravator condition) Third, was this murder especially heinous, atrocious or cruel? In this context heinous means extremely wicked or shockingly evil; atrocious means outrageously wicked and vile; and cruel means designed to inflict a high degree of pain with utter indifference to, or even enjoyment of, the suffering of others. However it is not enough that this murder be heinous, atrocious or cruel as those terms have just been defined. This murder must have been especially heinous, atrocious or cruel, and not every murder is especially so. For this murder to have been especially heinous, atrocious or cruel, any brutality which was involved in it must have exceeded that which is normally present in any killing, or this murder must have been a conscienceless or pitiless crime which was unnecessarily torturous to the victim. If you find from the evidence beyond a reasonable doubt that this aggravating circumstance exists, you would so indicate by writing, "Yes," in the space after this aggravating circumstance on the "Issues and Recommendation" form. If you do not so find, or have a reasonable doubt as to one or more of these things, you will write, "No," in that space.

Finally, was this murder part of a course of conduct in which the defendant engaged and did that course of conduct include the commission by the defendant of other crimes of violence against another person or persons? A murder is part of such a course of conduct if you find from the evidence beyond a reasonable doubt that, in addition to killing the victim, the defendant was engaged in a course of conduct which involved the commission of another crime of violence against another person. If you find this aggravating circumstance you would so indicate by writing, "Yes," in the space after this aggravating circumstance on the "Issues and Recommendation" form. If you do not find, or have a reasonable doubt as to one or more of these things, you will write, "No," in that space.

If you find from the evidence beyond a reasonable doubt that one or more of these aggravating circumstances existed, and have so indicated by writing, "Yes," in the space after one or more of them on the "Issues and Recommendation" form, you would answer Issue One, "Yes." On the other hand, if you find from the evidence that none of the aggravating circumstances existed, and if you have so indicated by writing, "No," in the space after every one of them on that form, you would answer Issue One, "No." If you answer Issue One, "No," you would skip Issues Two, Three and Four and you must recommend that the defendant be sentenced to life imprisonment. If you answer Issue One, "Yes," then you would consider Issue Two.

Issue Two is, "Do you find from the evidence the existence of one or more of the following mitigating circumstances?" The possible mitigating circumstances are listed on the form, and you should consider each of them before answering Issue Two.

A mitigating circumstance is a fact or group of facts, which do not constitute a justification or excuse for a killing, or reduce it to a lesser degree of crime than first degree murder, but which may be considered as extenuating or reducing the moral culpability of the killing or making it less deserving of extreme punishment than other first degree murders. Our law identifies several possible mitigating circumstances. The defendant has the burden of persuading you that a given mitigating circumstance exists. The existence of any mitigating circumstance must be established by a preponderance of the evidence, that is, the evidence, taken as a whole must satisfy you--not beyond a reasonable doubt, but simply satisfy you--that any mitigating circumstance exists. It is your duty to consider the following mitigating circumstances, and any of the circumstances that the defendant contends is a basis for a sentence less than death, and any other circumstances arising from the evidence which you deem to have mitigating value.

First, consider whether this murder was committed while the defendant was under the influence of mental or emotional disturbance. A defendant is under such influence if he is in any way affected or influenced by a mental or emotional disturbance at the time he kills. A person may be under the influence of mental or emotional disturbance even if he had no adequate provocation. For this mitigating circumstance to exist, it is enough that the defendant's mind or emotions were disturbed, from any cause, and that he was under the influence of the disturbance when he killed the victim. You would find this mitigating circumstance if you find that the defendant was upset because of his failing marriage, financial and employment difficulties, the fight between the defendant and his wife, or the fight between the defendant and the victim, and that the defendant was under the influence of emotional disturbance when he killed the victim. If you find by a preponderance of the evidence that this circumstance exists, you would so indicate by writing, "Yes," in the space provided after this mitigating circumstance on the "Issues and Recommendation" form. If you do not find this circumstance to exist, write "No," in that space.

(This mitigator only in the high mitigation condition) Second, consider whether the defendant testified truthfully on behalf of the prosecution in another prosecution of a felony. A defendant does so if he is called as a witness for the State at any stage of the prosecution of any felony and truthfully answers any questions asked by the prosecutor. The felony need not be connected with the murder for which you are recommending punishment. If you find by a preponderance of the evidence that the circumstance exists, you would so indicate by writing, "Yes," in the space provided after this mitigating circumstance on the "Issues and Recommendation" form. If you do not find this circumstance to exist, write, "No," in that space.

Next, consider whether the defendant is a good candidate for psychological rehabilitation. A defendant is a good candidate if it appears, to mental health professionals or to you as a juror that the defendant is likely to be able to successfully address his psychological problems and improve his mental health. If you find by a preponderance of the evidence that the circumstance exists, you would so indicate by writing, "Yes," in the space provided after this mitigating circumstance on the "Issues and Recommendation" form. If you do not find this circumstance to exist, write "No," in that space.

(This mitigator only in the high mitigation condition) Fourth, consider whether the defendant confessed and voluntarily cooperated with the police after the commission of the crime. You would find this circumstance if you find that the defendant willfully volunteered information about the crime, including that he had committed the crime and where the crime was committed. If you find by a preponderance of the evidence that the circumstance exists, you would so indicate by writing, "Yes," in the space provided after this mitigating circumstance on the "Issues and Recommendation" form. If you do not find this circumstance to exist, write "No," in that space.

Finally, you may consider any other circumstance or circumstances arising from the evidence which you deem to have mitigating value. If one or more of you so find by a preponderance of the evidence, you would so indicate by writing "Yes" in the space provided after this mitigating circumstance on the "Issues and Recommendations" form. If you do not find any such circumstance to exist, write "No" in that space.

If you find by a preponderance of the evidence one or more mitigating circumstances, and have so indicated by writing "Yes" in the space provided after this mitigating circumstance on the "Issues and Recommendation" form, you would answer Issue Two, "Yes." If you do not find any of these mitigating circumstances to exist and have so indicated by writing, "No," in the space after every one of them on that form, you would answer Issue Two, "No." If you answer Issue Two, "Yes," you must consider Issue Three. If you answer Issue Two, "No," do not answer Issue Three. Instead, skip Issue Three, and answer Issue Four.

Issue Three is, "Do you find beyond a reasonable doubt that the mitigating circumstance or circumstances found is, or are, insufficient to outweigh the aggravating circumstance or circumstances found by you?"

If you find from the evidence one or more mitigating circumstances, you must weigh the aggravating circumstance(s) against the mitigating circumstance(s). In so doing, you are the sole judge of the weight to be given to any individual circumstance which you find, whether aggravating or mitigating. You should not merely add up the number of aggravating circumstances and mitigating circumstances. Rather, you must decide from all the evidence what value to give to each circumstance, and then weigh the aggravating circumstances, so valued, against the mitigating circumstances, so valued, and finally determine whether the mitigating circumstances are insufficient to outweigh the aggravating circumstances.

If you find beyond a reasonable doubt that the mitigating circumstances found are insufficient to outweigh the aggravating circumstance(s) found, you would answer Issue Three, "Yes." If you fail to so find, you would answer Issue Three "No." If you answer Issue Three, "No," it would be your duty to recommend that the defendant be sentenced to life imprisonment. If you answer Issue Three, "Yes," you must consider Issue Four.

Issue Four is, "Do you find beyond a reasonable doubt that the aggravating circumstance or circumstances you found is, or are, sufficiently substantial to call for the imposition of the death penalty when considered with the mitigating circumstance or circumstances?"

In deciding this issue, you are not to consider the aggravating circumstances standing alone. You must consider them in connection with any mitigating circumstances you found. After considering the totality of the aggravating and mitigating circumstances, you must be convinced beyond a reasonable doubt that the imposition of the death penalty is justified and appropriate in this case before you can answer the issue "Yes." In so doing, you are not applying a mathematical formula. For example, three circumstances of one kind do not automatically and of necessity outweigh one circumstance of another kind. You may very properly give more weight to one circumstance than another. You must consider the relative substantiality and persuasiveness of the existing aggravating and mitigating circumstances in making this determination. In the event you do not find the existence of any mitigating circumstances, you must still answer this issue. In such case, you must determine whether the aggravating circumstances found by you are of such value, weight, importance, consequence, or significance as to be sufficiently substantial to call for the imposition of the death penalty. After so doing, if you find beyond a reasonable doubt that the aggravating circumstances found are sufficiently substantial to call for the death penalty when considered with mitigating circumstances, it would be your duty to answer the issue "Yes." If you fail to so find, it would be your duty to answer the issue "No."

If you answer Issue Four, "No," you must recommend that the defendant be sentenced to life imprisonment. If you answer Issue Four, "Yes," it would be your duty to recommend that the defendant be sentenced to death.

You have heard the evidence and the arguments of counsel for the State and for the defendant. It is your duty not only to consider all the evidence, but also to consider all the arguments, the contentions and positions urged by the State's attorney and the defendant's attorney in their speeches to you, and any other contention that arises from the evidence, and to weigh them in the light of your common sense, and to make your recommendation as to punishment. When you are ready to make a recommendation, write in your recommendation as directed on the "Issues and Recommendation" form.

APPENDIX D: VERDICT FORM

ISSUES AND RECOMMENDATION AS TO PUNISHMENT

ISSUE ONE

DO YOU FIND FROM THE EVIDENCE, BEYOND A
REASONABLE DOUBT, THE EXISTENCE OF ONE OR MORE OF
THE FOLLOWING AGGRAVATING CIRCUMSTANCES?
ANSWER: ______

The defendant had been previously convicted of a felony involving the
use or threat of violence to the person________

The capital felony was committed for pecuniary gain ______

The capital felony was especially heinous, atrocious, or cruel.______

The murder for which the defendant stands convicted was part of a
course of conduct in which the defendant engaged and which included
the commission by the defendant of other crimes of violence against
another person or persons ________

IF YOU WRITE, "YES", IN ONE OR MORE OF THE SPACES
AFTER THE AGGRAVATING CIRCUMSTANCES, WRITE, "YES"
IN THE SPACE AFTER ISSUE ONE AS WELL. IF YOU WRITE
"NO" IN ALL THE SPACES AFTER THE AGGRAVATING
CIRCUMSTANCES, WRITE "NO" IN THE SPACE AFTER ISSUE
ONE.

IF YOU ANSWERED ISSUE ONE "NO", SKIP ISSUES TWO,
THREE, AND FOUR, AND INDICATE LIFE IMPRISONMENT
UNDER "RECOMMENDATION AS TO PUNISHMENT," ON THE
LAST PAGE OF THIS FORM. IF YOU ANSWERED ISSUE ONE
"YES", PROCEED TO ISSUE TWO.

ISSUE TWO

DO YOU FIND FROM THE EVIDENCE THE EXISTENCE OF ONE OR MORE OF THE FOLLOWING MITIGATING CIRCUMSTANCES? ANSWER: ______.

The capital felony was committed while the defendant was under the influence of mental or emotional disturbance ______

The defendant testified truthfully on behalf of the prosecution in another trial of a felony______

The defendant is a good candidate for successful psychological rehabilitation ______

The defendant confessed to the crime and cooperated with authorities

______

Any other circumstance arising from the evidence which the jury deems to have mitigating value ______

IF YOU WRITE, "YES", IN ONE OR MORE OF THE SPACES AFTER THE MITIGATING CIRCUMSTANCES, WRITE, "YES" IN THE SPACE AFTER ISSUE ONE AS WELL. IF YOU WRITE "NO" IN ALL THE SPACES AFTER THE MITIGATING CIRCUMSTANCES, WRITE "NO" IN THE SPACE AFTER ISSUE ONE ABOVE. IF YOU ANSWERED ISSUE TWO "YES", THEN ANSWER ISSUE THREE. IF YOU ANSWERED ISSUE TWO "NO", THEN SKIP ISSUE THREE AND ANSWER ISSUE FOUR.

ISSUE THREE

DO YOU FIND BEYOND A REASONABLE DOUBT THAT THE MITIGATING CIRCUMSTANCE OR CIRCUMSTANCES ARE, INSUFFICIENT TO OUTWEIGH THE AGGRAVATING CIRCUMSTANCE OR CIRCUMSTANCES FOUND IN ISSUE ONE? ANSWER: ______.

IF YOU ANSWER ISSUE THREE "NO", THEN INDICATE LIFE IMPRISONMENT UNDER "RECOMMENDATIONS AS TO PUNISHMENT".

IF YOU ANSWER ISSUE THREE "YES", THEN PROCEED TO ISSUE FOUR.

ISSUE FOUR

DO YOU FIND BEYOND A REASONABLE DOUBT THAT THE AGGRAVATING CIRCUMSTANCE OR CIRCUMSTANCES FOUND IN ISSUE ONE IS, OR ARE, SUFFICIENTLY SUBSTANTIAL TO CALL FOR THE IMPOSITION OF THE DEATH PENALTY WHEN CONSIDERED WITH THE MITIGATING CIRCUMSTANCE OR CIRCUMSTANCES FOUND? ANSWER: ______.

IF YOU ANSWER ISSUE FOUR "NO", INDICATE LIFE IMPRISONMENT UNDER "RECOMMENDATION AS TO PUNISHMENT" ON THE LAST PAGE OF THIS FORM.

IF YOU ANSWER ISSUE FOUR "YES", INDICATE DEATH UNDER "RECOMMENDATION AS TO PUNISHMENT."

APPENDIX E: DEPENDENT MEASURES SURVEY

RECOMMENDATION AS TO PUNISHMENT

INDICATE YOUR RECOMMENDATION AS TO PUNISHMENT BY WRITING "LIFE IMPRISONMENT" OR "DEATH" IN THE BLANK IN THE FOLLOWING SENTENCE: I RECOMMEND THAT THE DEFENDANT, MICHAEL BRADLEY, BE SENTENCED TO ______________ (PLEASE FILL IN THE BLANK).

Please indicate your sentencing decision:

______Life Sentence without the possibility of parole

______ Death Penalty

How certain are you in your sentencing decision? Please circle one number:

VERY  1----2----3----4----5----6----7 VERY

UNCERTAIN                                CERTAIN

Instructions: Please indicate your answers to the following questions by circling ONE number.

1. How strongly do you agree that the defendant is guilty of first degree murder?

STRONGLY   1----2---3---4---5----6---7  STRONGLY

DISAGREE               Neutral                AGREE

2. Is your opinion concerning the death penalty based on your religious beliefs?

NOT   1---------2---------3------4-------5-------6-------7  YES

AT ALL                        Moderately              STRONGLY

3. State Law requires the death penalty in some cases.

___Yes ____No

4. Did the defense attorney give you Biblical examples of why you should forgive the defendant?  ____ yes ___ no

How did the defense attorney tell you to make the sentencing decision? (check all that apply)

5. ____ Use your gut instincts and feelings

6. ____ Ask other jurors

7. ____ Use your logic and reason

8. ____ Compare this crime to other crimes you have heard about

9. ____ Weigh the evidence for each side

Which, if any, of the following stories did the defense attorney tell in his closing argument? (check all, if any, that apply)

10. ___ Story about a man who killed his neighbor

11. ___ Story about Jesus being crucified

12. ___ Story about a woman killed during a bank robbery

13. ___ Story about a person killing a small child in the cruelest way possible

Instructions: The next question concerns what people or things of the case influenced your sentencing decision.  Please indicate how much each person or thing influenced your sentencing decision, using the following scale:

DID NOT INFLUENCE  1--2--3--4--5--6--7  STRONGLY

AT ALL                              Neutral        INFLUENCED

Write your answer (1-7) in the space next to each person or thing.


14. _____ Judges instructions/State law

15. _____ Biblical authority

16. _____ Defense attorney arguments

17. _____ Prosecution arguments

18. _____ Evidence presented in the case

19. _____ Your personal religious beliefs

20. _____ Your personal feelings about the death penalty

21. _____ My feelings about this case

22. _____ My instincts about this case

23. _____ My feelings about the defendant

24. _____ Logic and reason

25._____ Common sense

26. _____ Other (please specify _________________)

Instructions: The following questions concern which entities you feel are responsible for the sentence the defendant receives. Please indicate how much responsibility each person or thing has for the sentencing decision, using the following scale:

NOT 1-----2-----3----4----5----6----7 VERY

RESPONSIBLE  neutral    RESPONSIBLE

Write the number of your answer (1-7) in the space next to each person or thing.

27. _____Judge's instructions/ state law

28. _____Biblical authority

29. _____Juror (you)

30. _____Defendant

31. _____Chance

32. _____The victim

33. _____ other (please specify_________________)

34. Are there any other factors that influenced your sentencing decision?          If          so,          please          explain:
_______________________________________________________

_______________________________________________________

Instructions: please rate your agreement with the next set of statements using the following scale

STRONGLY   1-----2-----3---4---5--6---7 STRONGLY

DISAGREE                    Neutral                    AGREE

Write the number of your answer (1-7) in the space beside each statement.

35. _____ Criminals should be forgiven for their acts.

36. _____ Criminals should be shown mercy.

37. _____ Criminals should receive "payback" for committing crimes.

38. _____ Murderers deserve the death penalty because they killed.

39._____ It is acceptable (i.e. appropriate) to invoke religion in the context of a criminal trial.

40. ____ God allows mercy for those who commit crimes.

41. ____ God allows forgiveness for those who commit crimes.

42. ____ The law allows mercy for those who commit crimes.

43. ____ The law allows forgiveness for those who commit crimes.

44. _____ God requires the death penalty for murderers.

45. _____God supports, but does not require the death penalty for murderers.

46. If you feel that God requires the death penalty for murderers, does the requirement of the death penalty apply to all murders equally, no matter what characteristics of the crime or the defendant?

___Yes ___ No

Instructions: Please answer the following questions about yourself:

47. Have you ever served as a juror on a real trial?

_____ Yes_____No

48. If yes, how many times?

_____Civil trial _______Criminal trial

49. Age _________

50. Gender: (check one) ________Male ________Female

51. Are you a student? ______Yes _____No

52.    If    yes,    what    is    your    major    course    of
     study?_______________________________________

53. What is your racial/ethnic background?

_____African-American               _____Native American

_____Asian-American                 _____White American

_____Hispanic-American              _____Other (please specify
                                            (_________)

54. What is your religious background?

________ Catholic: please specify ______________________________

______Protestant: please specify (e.g. Baptist, Methodist)
     _________________________________________________

______ Jewish: please specify (e.g. orthodox, reformed)
     _________________________________________________

______ Hindu

______Buddhist

______Muslim

______Other (please specify _______________________________)

68_____ I believe there is a Divine plan and purpose for every living person and thing.

69._____ The only benefit one receives from prayer is psychological.

70. _____ I have a duty to help those who are confused about religion.

71. _____ Even though it may create some unpleasant situations, it is important to help others become enlightened about religion.

72. _____ There is no point in arguing about religion, because there is little chance of changing other people's minds.

73. _____ It doesn't really matter what an individual believes about religion as long as he is happy with it.

74. _____ I believe the world would really be a better place if more people held the views about religion, which I hold.

75. _____ I believe the world's problems are seriously aggravated by the fact that so many people are misguided about religion.

76. Have you ever tried to encourage someone to believe in Jesus Christ or to accept Jesus Christ as his or her savior?

_____Yes _____No

77. Do you believe that the Bible is the actual word of God and is to be taken literally, word for word?

_____ Yes _____No

Instructions: The following are some statements that may or may not be true of you and your character. Please indicate if the statements are true or false using the following scale:

COMPLETELY 1-----2----3----4-----5 COMPLETELY

FALSE                                                          TRUE

Please write the number of your answer (1-5) in the space beside each statement:

Please note: This scale is from 1-5, so your answers should NOT be above 5.

78. _____ I don't like to have to do a lot of thinking.

79. _____ I try to avoid situations that require thinking in depth about something.

80. _____ I prefer to do something that challenges my thinking abilities rather than something that requires little thought.

81. _____ I prefer complex to simple problems.

82. _____ Thinking hard and for a long time about something gives me little satisfaction.

83. _____ I trust my initial feelings about people.

84. _____ I believe in trusting my hunches.

85. _____ My initial impressions of people are almost always right.

86. _____ When it comes to trusting people, I can usually rely on my "gut feelings."

87. _____ I can usually feel when a person is right or wrong even if I can't explain how I know.

APPENDIX F: CEST MEASURES

Please read the following paragraph carefully and answer the question that follows.

> Linda is 31 years old, single, outspoken and very bright. She majored in philosophy. As a student, she was deeply concerned with issues of discrimination and social justice, and also participated in anti-nuclear demonstrations.

Following are several statements that may or may not be true of Linda. Please rank the statements according to the degree to which you believe Linda resembles the typical member of that class. For example, put a 1 by the statement you feel is most likely to be true, a 2 by the statement you feel is second most likely to be true, and so on up to the number 8, which is the statement you feel is least likely to be true.

You will only use each number (1-8) once!

_______ Linda is a teacher in elementary school.

_______ Linda works in a bookstore and takes Yoga classes.

_______ Linda is active in the feminist movement.

_______ Linda is a psychiatric social worker.

_______ Linda is a member of the League of Women Voters.

_______ Linda is a bank teller.

_______ Linda is an insurance salesperson.

_______ Linda is a bank teller and is active in the feminist movement.

Mr. Paul, who has an average income, owned shares in company A. During the past year he switched to stock in company B., He has just learned that the stock in A has skyrocketed, and he would now be $100,000 ahead if he had kept his stock in company A.

Mr. George, who also has an average income, owns shares in company B. During the past year he considered switching stock to company A, but decided against it. He has just learned that stock in A skyrocketed and he would now be $100,000 ahead if he had made the switch.

Who do you think was more foolish, Mr. Paul or Mr. George?

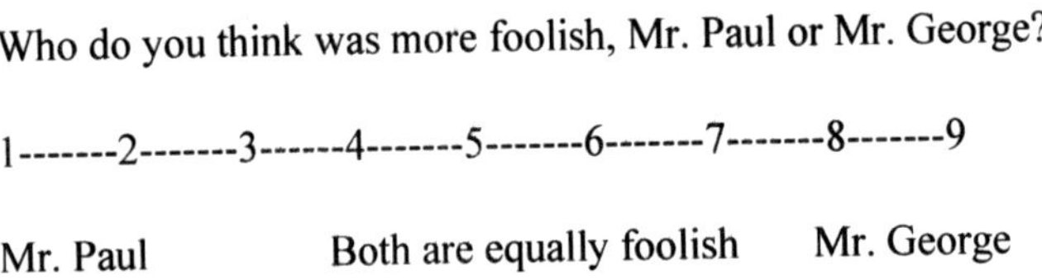

1-------2-------3------4-------5-------6-------7-------8------9

Mr. Paul                Both are equally foolish      Mr. George

Tom parked his new car in a parking lot that was half empty. His wife asked him to park in a spot where she wanted to shop, but he parked, instead, in a spot closer to where he wanted to shop. As luck would have it, when he backed out after shopping, another car opposite to him backed out at the same time and both cars sustained damage over $1,000.

Robert parked his new car in the same parking lot when there was only one parking place, so he took it. As luck would have it, when he backed out after shopping, another car opposite to him backed out at the same time and both cars sustained damage over $1,000.

Who do you think contributed more to the likelihood of the accident, and therefore is more foolish, Tom or Robert?

1-------2-------3------4-------5-------6-------7-------8------9

Tom                    Both are equally foolish              Robert

# APPENDIX G: DEATH QUALIFICATION MEASURES

This questionnaire is designed to learn about your attitude toward the death penalty. There are no right answers and there are no wrong answers. Some people are in favor of the death penalty and some are opposed to it. Neither position is the correct position. This questionnaire simply asks you two questions. The first asks your opinion about the topic and the second asks how you would conduct yourself if you were a juror. For each question read the statements completely and then check the one statement that best describes what your attitude would be if you were a juror in a death penalty case. Your answer will be completely confidential. At no time will your answer be connected to your name.

Question 1: What is your attitude toward the death penalty? (check one of the following):

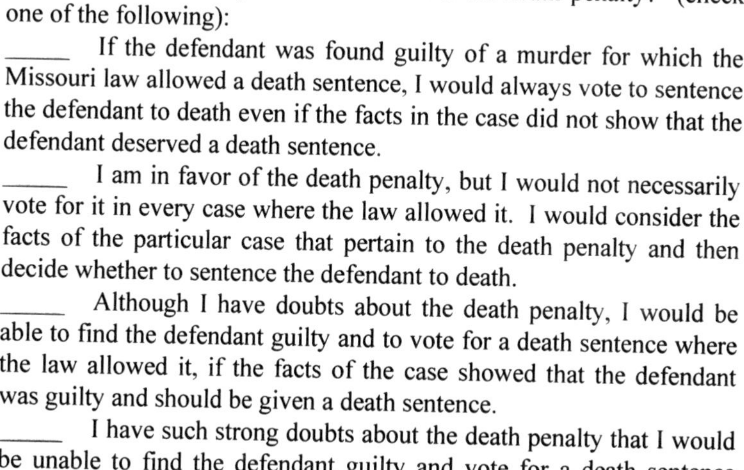

______ If the defendant was found guilty of a murder for which the Missouri law allowed a death sentence, I would always vote to sentence the defendant to death even if the facts in the case did not show that the defendant deserved a death sentence.

______ I am in favor of the death penalty, but I would not necessarily vote for it in every case where the law allowed it. I would consider the facts of the particular case that pertain to the death penalty and then decide whether to sentence the defendant to death.

______ Although I have doubts about the death penalty, I would be able to find the defendant guilty and to vote for a death sentence where the law allowed it, if the facts of the case showed that the defendant was guilty and should be given a death sentence.

______ I have such strong doubts about the death penalty that I would be unable to find the defendant guilty and vote for a death sentence where the law allowed it, even if the facts of the case showed that the defendant was guilty and deserved a death sentence.

Question 2: Given your position regarding the death penalty, which of the following statements best describes how you would conduct yourself as a jury on a capital murder case? (check one):

______     I have such strong sentiments about the death penalty that they would seriously affect me as a juror and would prevent or substantially impair my performance in accordance with my instructions and oath.

______     My sentiments about the death penalty are not so strong that they would seriously affect me as a juror and would prevent or substantially impair my performance in accordance with my instructions and oath.

# Index